SPIRIT
OF THE BADGE

SPIRIT
OF THE BADGE

60 TRUE POLICE STORIES *of*
Divine Guidance, Miracles, & Intuition

INGRID P. DEAN

TOPAZ HEART PUBLISHING
Traverse City, Michigan

Topaz Heart Publishing, LLC
www.spiritofthebadge.com

Dean, Ingrid P.

Spirit of the badge : 60 true police stories of divine guidance, miracles, & intuition / Ingrid P. Dean — Traverse City, Mich. : Topaz Heart Pub., c2009.

p. ; ill. cm.

ISBN: 978-0-9820824-0-9

1. Police psychology. 2. Police—United States—Attitudes. 3. Gifts, Spiritual. I. Title.

HV7936.P75 D43 2009   2008909342
363.2019—dc22   0904

Printed in the United States of America
10 9 8 7 6 5 4 3 2

Cover photo by Karin Willman
www.printroom.com/pro/alacarte

Cover design and interior layout by To The Point Solutions
www.tothepointsolutions.com

To Michael Curtis, my uncle and a famous artist,
who told me long ago that color was nothing but refracted light
to be spread to the world unconditionally by all.

Contents

Angels & Apparitions

Dreams & Intuition

Healing With Humor

Lessons of the Heart

Symbols, Signs, & Synchronicity

Unexplainable Phenomena

Preface

"A human being is part of the whole, called by us 'universe,' a part limited in time and space. He experiences his thoughts and feelings as something separate from the rest—a kind of optical delusion of his consciousness. This delusion is a kind of prison for us, restricting us to our personal decisions and to affection for a few persons nearest us. Our task must be to free ourselves from this prison by widening our circle of compassion to embrace all living creatures and the whole of nature in its beauty."

Albert Einstein

The experience of interconnected consciousness has been held as significant for thousands of years, yet it is not accepted as a mutually agreed upon reality. Because of irresolvable personal, religious, and intellectual conflicts—stemming from deeply held convictions about the makeup of life—we have only gradually developed ways of exploring the truth of our innermost nature.

This book is a creative compilation of unusual, moving, and exceptional moments experienced by police officers in their daily work. These moments imply we are interconnected. Law enforcement officers represent a small portion of our world population, but like other groups and professional families, they are sometimes regarded negatively as *separate, apart, robotic, authoritarian, ego-maniacs*, etc.—I could come up with many more adjectives that are pejorative.

I suggest that police officers are not separate from you. Police officers are human beings who, consciously or unconsciously, choose to serve people for the common good. Hence, this heartfelt collection of true stories is an attempt to help untangle some of the illusory misconceptions and boundaries that have been created between police officers and the general public.

I believe that our goal as a human race is to share a greater sense of belonging together and to realize that we are all interrelated. If we are able to heighten our sense of connection to a larger whole, then a new level of shared intelligence, respect, compassion, and creativity will begin to emerge among everyone.

May we all contribute to the common goal of oneness in some small way. Thank you to all my fellow police associates and friends who entrusted me with their remarkable stories.

In heartfelt gratitude,

Ingrid

Acknowledgments

Publication of this book was made possible by the collective contributions of many active and retired police officers, their friends, and families. Special thanks are due to the Michigan Department of State Police and Retired Colonel Tadarial Sturdivant for supporting and approving my request to research police experiences for my Master's Degree in Transpersonal Studies. This book is the final result of an exciting, atypical, culminating school project.

My heartfelt thanks to all the law enforcement officers and staff from agencies around the country who contributed personal interviews, written letters, emails, and photographs to produce this extraordinary collection of stories. The camaraderie and enthusiasm among police officers never ceases to amaze me. I was contacted by many officers I had never met before, in addition to those I was acquainted with. I can not express enough thanks and gratitude to all of you for your honesty, courage, and openness in sharing such personal experiences for people to read. Thank you for granting me your permission to print stories that are so rarely shared with the public. You have been my greatest street teachers for almost twenty years!

Blessings to all the academic teachers in my life, who encouraged and supported me throughout this project: Drs. Frank and Shelley Takai, Drs. Mark and Mary Thurston, Dr. Henry Reed, and Greg Deming. I am especially grateful to Dr. Michael Mirdad, who came up with excellent ideas for my initial research project and who unconditionally served as an energetic healer and teacher to me for the last four years.

Many thanks to all of my spiritual life teachers, past and present, who directly, indirectly, and synchronistically contributed their energy and strength for this book to happen. I am indebted to my oldest hands-on spiritual teachers, Michael and Beth Stone, who prepared me to write a book like this. Most recently, I thank Bodhi Avinasha, Larry Melamerson, Richard and Antoinette Asimus, and again, Michael Mirdad, for their insights into Kriya Yoga and spiritual awareness. Through yoga they have taught me the value of circulating life force energy for personal healing and rejuvenation. Without them, I'm not sure this book would have ever happened!

I sincerely thank my mother, Dr. Caroline Dunlap, for the initial editing she provided.

I thank my sister, Ellen Driesbaugh, and my best friend, Linda McCleary, for their enthusiasm, support, and insight.

And special thanks to Mary Jo Zazueta of To the Point Solutions, who edited the final manuscript and beautifully designed, in style and composition, both my school presentation and this final publication.

Contributors

In addition to the author, the following law enforcement officers and advocates, active and retired, contributed one or more stories to this publication. The author gratefully acknowledges these individuals for permission to include their material and also thanks those whose stories did not get selected due to space and other considerations.

CHARLES ALLEN, Inspector, Michigan State Police, Saginaw, Michigan

ROBERT I. ARCINIEGA, Trooper, Retired, Michigan State Police, Traverse City, Michigan

JOHN G. ARTHUR, Trooper, Michigan State Police, Traverse City, Michigan

LAWRENCE A. BAK, Detective Sergeant, Michigan State Police, Alpena, Michigan

SCOTT R. BATES, Trooper, Michigan State Police, Houghton Lake, Michigan

MONICA BRADFORD, Sergeant, Michigan State Police, Traverse City, Michigan

RAYMOND BRONICKI, Trooper, Retired, Michigan State Police, Niles, Michigan

THOMAS A. BROSMAN III, X50, Senior Telecommunications Specialist, Washington State Police, Tacoma, Washington

HERMAN BROWN, Trooper, Michigan State Police, Monroe, Michigan

DANIEL J. CAVISTON, Detective Sergeant, Retired, Michigan State Police, Traverse City, Michigan

CARY J. CLARK, Trooper, Michigan State Police, Detroit, Michigan

Contributors

THOMAS M. CURTIS, Lieutenant, Retired, Michigan State Police, Fenton, Michigan

MARK A. DAVID, Detective, Oscoda Township Police, Oscoda, Michigan

ROBERT DYKSTRA, Detective Lieutenant, Michigan State Police, Northville, Michigan

SARAH FOSTER, Trooper, Michigan State Police, Livonia, Michigan

KENNETH C. GOLAT, Chief, Manistique Public Safety, Manistique, Michigan

MARY GROENEVELD, Trooper, Michigan State Police, Iron Mountain, Michigan

MICHAEL HANCOCK, Officer, Retired, Grandville Police Department, Grandville, Michigan

JORDON HARTLEY, Detective, Mason County Sheriff Department, Ludington, Michigan

TODD M. HELLER, Detective, Grand Traverse Sheriff Department, Traverse City, Michigan

CRAIG W. JOHNSON, Trooper, Michigan State Police, West Branch, Michigan

REUBEN R. JOHNSON, Detective Lieutenant, Retired, Michigan State Police, Lake City, Michigan

BOBIE JOHNSTON, Officer, Mackinac Island Police Department, Mackinac Island, Michigan

DUANE H. LEROY, JR., Chief, Retired, Leslie Police Department, Leslie, Michigan

ROBERT MARBLE, Trooper, Michigan State Police, Manistee, Michigan

GARY MCGHEE, Captain, Retired, Michigan State Police, Interlochen, Michigan

CHARLES W. NEWSOME, Officer, Retired, Detroit Police Department, Riverview, Michigan

LARRY D. NICHOLS, Chief of Police, Scottville Police Department, Scottville, Michigan

DANIEL O'RILEY, Detective Lieutenant, Wexford County Sheriff Department, Cadillac, Michigan

VERNON PETERSEN, Detective Lieutenant, Retired, Michigan State Police, Marquette, Michigan

GLENN SANFORD, Trooper, Retired, Michigan State Police, Traverse City, Michigan

STEPHEN C. SOKOL, Officer, Detroit Police Department, Detroit, Michigan

LEONARD A. SPECKIN, First Lieutenant, Retired, Michigan State Police, Okemos, Michigan

STEVEN R. STANDFEST, Lieutenant, Retired, Beverly Hills Department of Public Safety, Hartland, Michigan

MICHAEL THOMAS, Captain, Michigan State Police, Lansing, Michigan

MICHAEL THOMAS, Officer, Retired, Flint Police Department, Flint, Michigan

DAWN WAGONER, Detective, Grand Traverse Sheriff Department, Traverse City, Michigan

MICHAEL W. WHEAT, Detective, Charlevoix Sheriff Department, Charlevoix, Michigan

ALAN L. WHITE, Officer, Clare Police Department, Clare, Michigan

DUANE WRIGHT, Deputy, Leelanau County Sheriff Department, Suttons Bay, Michigan

"At present, people create barriers between each other by their fragmentary thought. Each one operates separately. When these barriers have dissolved, then there arises one mind, where they are all one unit, but each person also retains his or her own individual awareness. That one mind will still exist when they are separate, and when they come together, it will be as if they hadn't separated . . . it's actually a single intelligence that works with people who are moving in relationship with one another . . . if you had a number of people who really pulled together and worked together in this way, it would be so remarkable."

David Bohm, Quantum Physicist

Introduction

The most fundamental questions of human existence are explored in what is regarded as the *transpersonal perspective*. Such questions include: What is the relationship of the personal to the transpersonal? What is the relationship of self to spirit? And, what is the nature of this relationship? As a result, the transpersonal perspective has become a fusion of wisdom collected from spiritual-world traditions with some of the philosophical and psychological schools of the West.

The transpersonal perspective, simply put, explores "beyond the person." It suggests that there is much about human beings that goes far beyond our five physical senses and that our soul, or consciousness, is much bigger than we realize. This new perspective is a way of organizing our experience of reality—it is not that reality itself.

Human consciousness is the term used to embody this synthesis of spiritual wisdom, philosophy, and psychology and moves beyond the confines of the self or soul. In moving beyond the confines of self, consciousness is seen to open up into ranges of human experience that go far beyond Freud's earlier formulations of id, ego, and superego. Consciousness becomes an expression for a vast multi-dimensional existence wherein new aspects of being are discovered.

Law enforcement officers often experience both ordinary and extraordinary situations that require or encourage a stretch in their personal decision-making and practices. Officers are called upon to protect, defend, support, manage, and save lives—including their own. They are expected to accomplish impossible feats and are criticized when they fail. Many would agree that such heavy responsibilities enhance policemen's awareness and senses, even when they don't realize it. Because of this heightened awareness, police build emotional armor to desensitize and numb themselves. It is a defense mechanism that manifests in their experiences so they don't have to feel so much. This may be why officers sometimes appear callous, frozen, and unwavering.

The "CSI Effect" is an interesting concept to explore. It is in reference to the phenomenon of popular television police shows that tend to raise the real-world expectations of forensic science and police work. From a transpersonal and psychological point of view, the "CSI Effect" encourages people into believing that only science will solve a serious offense. Thus, prosecutors are pressured to deliver more and more forensic scientific evidence in court, often inapplicable to the case, and less weight is given to anything else considered relevant or important for a jury to hear.

Most police experts would agree that good detectives solve crimes by looking at all of the angles in a case. Hence, television shows like *CSI* often narrow, if not outright abolish, people's ideas that there could be any methods of proof other than scientific—such as observation, intuition, right listening, or cognitive interviewing.

Solving a crime is both an art and a science, combined to produce a fuller and more accurate picture of an alleged occurrence. Investigative work isn't "just the facts, ma'am, just the facts." I have heard officers say time and time again, "Thank God for gut instinct!"

The majority of committed, dedicated, and devoted police officers—regardless of their public image—will do whatever it takes to assist and resolve a traumatic or threatening situation, to the point that they go beyond self. They will go beyond their five physical senses—even if it entails a near-death experience. Psychic ability, intuition, and gut-instinct are not unique gifts or paranormal capacities but rather abilities and skills that anyone can develop with practice. Everyone can discover and develop his or her transpersonal talents and inner wisdom using intuition, logic, and common sense in order to make the best choices.

By and by, police officers are honest, decent, dignified folks who want nothing more than to do noble things for people. They seldom run out and capitalize on the good things they do because then their motives for sharing are challenged. Ultimately, police officers are no different than anyone else. Everyone likes to receive some occasional validation. In my opinion, however, police officers do not get much validation because people forget they are human.

The public gets caught up in the stereotypical image of what a policeman should be, based on what is depicted and expressed on television. The public only sees cops in dramatic Hollywood stories and gets an inaccurate perception of who the human being is behind the badge. Thus, we have done nothing more than build stereotypes that have become part of our collective consciousness of a public who wants to see through the cops' eyes but gets little exposure to the reality and truth of their humaneness.

The first two decades of the transpersonal field largely focused on the high end of human experience. In the formative years, the transpersonal perspective was often thought of, exclusively, as anything beyond normal human comprehension, such as altered states of consciousness, extrasensory perception, near-death experiences, astral vision, and other intuitive states. These examples do shape a significant part of the transpersonal perspective; however, such incidents are becoming less of a focus now as the transpersonal perspective expands and advances towards a more complete and all-inclusive view of the human heart and experience.

This book is a reflective and unusual examination of unexplainable situations and phenomena. The stories imply a greater force or intelligence within and beyond ourselves, which we have, perhaps, not explored enough. Additionally, many stories show good quality police work that is a result of highly developed skills in awareness, attention to detail, and in noticing things out of place or "not right."

Interestingly, the officers who submitted their stories were perfectionists to a fault. Like a police report, their stories had to be accurate and were corrected if only one word was off. I consider all these police extremely credible and am honored that they shared their experiences with me.

I ask you, the reader, to consider the possibility that we are all experiencing a shift in paradigm, not only in law enforcement, but in other professions and within our own collective consciousness. Consequently, more and more reliable and believable professionals are starting to acknowledge extraordinary experiences that imply a compassionate interconnectedness among people.

Lastly, it is my hope and prayer that readers will gain a deeper understanding and appreciation for the psychological, emotional, and spiritual aspects of police officers. I believe that police officers, their departments, and society in general are entering into a new era for the criminal justice system. The new era not only includes cutting-edge technologies and practical, client-based, problem-solving approaches to law enforcement, but also includes a developing appreciation and respect for the more receptive, intuitive, and creative aspects of police officers who have to deal directly with the human condition. Police work does go beyond "just the facts, ma'am."

This book will demonstrate that reality.

SPIRIT
OF THE BADGE

Angels & Apparitions

Shared observances and interactions with angels and apparitions are valuable because they expand our grasp of possibility. While death may remain a physical reality from a scientific point of view, these recorded experiences lessen the sting and fear of death. That is what makes these encounters so transpersonal.

"Angels are messengers,
but sometimes we misunderstand their language."

Linda Solegato

"An angel is someone who helps you
believe in miracles again."

Author Unknown

An Angel's Shield

In 1992, I worked the 12th precinct (now the Western District) of the city of Detroit in a marked uniformed patrol unit. My regular partner and I had been separated by a shift supervisor who didn't like either one of us. I was paired with a desk officer who had little street experience. As we went out on the road, I hoped it was going to be an average day.

As it became dark, we found ourselves driving north on Wyoming Road near Santa Clara. There was a red light at the intersection and all traffic was stopped. The car in front of us was occupied by three guys and had license plate BNL661 (I'll never forget that number). The car stopped momentarily and then drove through the light. My first thought was that the light was stuck, but then it turned green.

The occupants of nearby cars looked at my partner and me as if to say, "You're the police. Do something about it."

We activated our lights and attempted to pull the car over. The occupants began to argue. We could see them yelling at each other. They weren't going fast; they were just cruising. But they weren't stopping the car either.

I advised our dispatcher of the situation and the direction we were traveling. The car turned down a side street and parked. Instinct told me to stay further behind than I normally would on a traffic stop.

As I started to exit the patrol car, the person in the front passenger seat leaned out of the door window and fired at me with an Intra-tech 9mm Uzi-style weapon.

Everything happened so fast, he fired at least three shots before I realized we were under fire. I quickly re-entered the police car to get to the radio to call for help. I shouted, "Officer in trouble! Twelve-11 under fire!" As I reached for my weapon, I could see bullets tearing through the metal hood of the patrol car on an angle toward the driver's door—my side. I knew if I exited I'd be hit.

Then the gunman fired a shot directly into the windshield of the patrol car at face level. I should have been killed. It should have hit me directly in the mouth. However, the bullet flew up, deflecting off the windshield. I knew the windshield wouldn't take another hit without being penetrated. I had no choice but to get out of the car to fire because my shots were not effective from a seated position.

As I started to leave the car, everything went into slow motion. I saw a golden light fill the car and heard a voice say, "Don't worry. You're going to come out of this fine. You won't be hurt." It was a calm male voice. I believed the voice. It felt as if a shield had been raised up in front of me. I knew that I wouldn't be hurt!

I exited the police car. The gunman was still shooting. I aimed and fired my weapon, causing the driver to floor the car and speed away. I emptied my magazine as the gunman and his accomplices fled. I was not harmed at all.

I looked around and saw my partner's hat in the street; the passenger door was wide open. The first thing I thought was that my partner was hit. I searched around the patrol car and advised dispatch that I couldn't find my partner. Moments later, additional police cars arrived, one with my partner in the backseat. It turned out my partner ran from the gunmen after the first shot.

Physically, I had been left alone—but spiritually I had the best backup in the world. I am alive today because of divine intervention.

Free As a Bird

My mother, whom I loved dearly, passed away at the age of sixty-two. She was a lifelong smoker, which severely impaired her health during the last ten years of her life. She suffered through several strokes, open-heart surgery, and other major health problems. Eventually she was homebound; connected to a thirty-foot air line and nasal cannula.

My father had passed away, so Mom lived alone. Basically all she could do for entertainment was read or watch television. To give her something to do, I bought a bird feeder and birdhouse and hung them in the tree that stood in front of her kitchen window. Her favorite pastime soon became sitting on a stool in the kitchen to watch the birds—some days for hours at a time.

She enjoyed watching the many different birds that came to the feeder. Her favorite were the chickadees. They were always so busy and happy—and they traveled in groups. Whenever I came over for coffee, Mom would tell me how she loved the chickadees best. During one of our last conversations before her death, she told me that she wanted to be one of them—she was tired of being tied down and wanted to be as free as a bird. This was early November.

A few days before Thanksgiving, Mom became very ill. She did not want to go to the hospital because she felt she would not come home this time. I basically forced her to go to emergency; where she was admitted into the hospital.

My nephew, Jason, had come down from Marquette to go deer hunting with me. Jason was only fifteen and never had a father. He had a difficult life, so as his uncle, I acted as his father figure and had gotten him addicted to deer hunting. When Jason arrived I told him that his grandmother was very ill and that we probably would not go hunting. Jason was disappointed but said he understood.

We went to the hospital and visited Mom. Before I went in the room, I spoke with a nurse who was also a personal friend. She told me that my mother was failing and that she would probably pass away in three to seven days. Jason and I then visited with Mom separately, for about an hour apiece. When I spoke with Mom, she said worriedly, "Ken, this time it is different. What is happening to me?"

Although I tried to make her feel better, she told me she thought she was dying. She then asked if I was going to take Jason hunting that day. I told her no. It was windy, dark, and miserable outside. We would just stay in town and then come back later in the afternoon to visit her again. Mom insisted I take Jason hunting, stating it was her wish that I do so and that I was not going to disappoint him or her. She told me point blank to leave, go hunting, and that when we came back later we had better have a deer hunting story for her.

I hugged and kissed Mom good-bye and left, promising to do as she asked.

I told Jason that we had been ordered by Grandma to go hunting. Jason was happy about this; even though I told him her situation was dire. Jason loved his grandmother—and he would be sad when she died—but her death had been expected several times during the past few years. We agreed to follow Mom's orders.

When we reached the woods I sent Jason down the trail by himself, to a deer blind I had prepared for him earlier that fall. To make him feel better, I told Jason I was also going to hunt, but that I wanted to stay near the car. After he was out of sight, I sat on the hood of the car, thinking about Mom and our life together. I did not get my gun out as hunting was the last thing on my mind.

I had parked the car in the middle of a small field. After about an hour, the weather abruptly changed from dark and dismal to bright and sunny with a light breeze. I spotted a lone bird flying across the field toward my car. As it came closer, I was amazed. It was a chickadee, about the size of a robin, which is huge for this type of bird.

The chickadee flew right to the car and landed next to me on the hood. It then flitted around the car, perching on the hood next to me several times. It would not leave. Eventually I found myself talking to the bird. The situation was extremely odd; the size of the bird, the fact that it was alone, and that it was so friendly and unafraid.

After a time, I heard a motor and saw a truck coming down the road. I recognized it as belonging to my best friend, Charlie Willour. I instantly knew why Charlie was there. Mom must have died.

As Charlie drove up, the chickadee flew in front of my face and then left. Charlie got out of this truck and gave me the news I expected hear: Mom had died about one hour earlier.

I knew my mother had visited me for the last time. She had come to say good-bye and to assure me that she was happy and at last as free as a bird. There is absolutely no doubt in my mind that freedom for some does come in death.

In loving memory of Trooper Robert Marble, who recently passed away in an off-duty traffic accident.

An Angel's Warning

When I was young, my mom said she had a guardian angel to watch over us especially whenever we traveled or did something risky, like race motorcycles. She said she always sent along her angel to take care of us.

Both of my parents died in 1987; my dad from a long battle with cancer, my mom of a broken heart (they died within twelve hours of each other). Since then, I have always known that my mom's angel watches over us, and I have called upon her many times to protect my own kids.

In 1997, another trooper and I from the Detroit Post volunteered to transfer to Benton Harbor. I figured Benton Harbor would be a lot like Detroit, plus it would be a break from the regular stuff at the Detroit Post.

Benton Harbor *was* a lot like Detroit, just on a smaller scale. One common practice was that when we came to a red light while patrolling, if traffic was clear we treated the light like a stop sign—stop, look both ways, and then drive through. The philosophy was get the job done, don't waste time sitting at a red light.

On one particular night I was driving, and we had been stop-signing red lights all night. About three in the morning, my partner and I approached a green light at a blind intersection in downtown Benton Harbor. The tall buildings on all corners prevented me from seeing any possible oncoming cars. I said to my partner, "We've been going through red lights all night, I think I'll stop for this green light and balance the scale." I had no sooner stopped at the light when a car came screaming around the corner, driving at a high rate of speed through the red light!

If I had not stopped at the green light, we would have been broadsided. My partner and I looked at each other in amazement. Both of our jaws were dropped as we stared at each other in awe. We both knew we had been divinely protected. I knew my mom's angel had saved me once again. (Of course, we chased down the car and took appropriate action.)

Spirits of the North

I've never been what you might call "poltergeist inclined." I enjoy a good horror movie as much as the next person, but I always dismissed alleged true tales of wandering spirits as figments of overactive imaginations. I always believed each strange occurrence had at least one logical explanation.

This was, of course, before I began working the late-night shift in City Hall at Skagway, Alaska.

Skagway's City Hall and police department are housed in the McCabe College Building. The local court, Magistrate's office, and Trail of 98 Museum also share the space. This grand old structure was built in 1900 as a woman's college and was, for a time, the only granite building in Alaska.

As with any old building, it had the obligatory creeks, groans, and murmurs. Unfortunately, no one bothered to tell me it was haunted. I say this now with some certainty, even though it may damage any reputation I have left as being a practical man.

After a break-in period, my first duty assignment was working the midnight shift. Sitting in the office during the wee hours, I would occasionally hear a few strange noises, but never gave them much thought. One early morning, however, changed my perception of what goes bump in the night—forever.

I was working on some much-neglected paperwork at my desk. The building was silent except for the faint hum of the Macintosh computer and my fingers performing a slow dance on the keyboard. Fighting off sleepiness caused by a daytime person trying to be nocturnal, I struggled with a rather boring theft report.

I had nearly completed the narrative when I heard a door

close. The door was in a rear hallway off of the court chambers. I recognized this door because of the many times I'd heard it close before. It was attached to a police storage room where uniforms and other equipment were kept. The solid oak door was at least two inches thick. An ancient brass knob and lock-set hinted at its age. The door would not stay open on its own and, if not held, would quickly slam shut behind you. As the door was swinging it made the most hideous screeching sound.

After hearing the door close, my first thought was that someone was in or had been in the storage room. This idea was quickly dismissed because the entire building was dark when I arrived. My second thought was that someone left the door propped open and whatever was holding it gave way.

I wasn't the least bit nervous as I rose from the desk and confidently walked through the dark courtroom and into the even darker hallway. After some fumbling around I turned on the hall light and approached the storage room door. I pulled on the knob and found it properly latched. Upon opening the door, the equipment room was dark, as it should be. I turned on the light and all of the contents seemed to be in order. I turned off the light and let the door shut on its own and was treated to the loud screeching and confident slam. Before walking away, I pulled on the knob one more time. It was locked. Satisfied, I returned to my desk and began making finishing touches to the report.

A few minutes later, I again heard the loud screech and the finality of the door slamming shut. This made the hair on the back of my neck rise to attention. Spooks were not on my mind at this point. I knew SOMEONE must have opened the door.

I pulled my weapon and made my way back to the dark courtroom using my best there-might-be-a-bad-guy-on-the-premises stalking maneuvers. I listened for signs of an intruder. As I crouched outside the door, all was silent in the hallway. My left hand reached for the light switch and the bulb snapped into action. I pounced forward, gun pointing down the hall, prepared for whoever was breaking in or out.

The hallway was empty. It then occurred to me that whoever opened the door must be hiding in the storage room. Using the before-mentioned police maneuvers, I opened the storage room door. No one.

I carefully looked around the assorted boxes and racks, satisfied that I was, in fact, alone. Somewhat relieved, I stepped back into the hallway and secured my weapon. I opened and closed the door several times, performing the "this can't be happening" test. Each time the door securely latched and held.

I even tried leaving the door shut and unlatched, and discovered that it would stay resting against the casing. Then, shutting the door with a forceful push, I pulled the knob as hard as I dared, making sure it was properly latched. I returned to my desk feeling confident all was in order. As I settled into my chair, the door screeched. This time, I was scared. My previous search had confirmed that no *living* being was stalking City Hall, which left only one possible explanation. Since the door could not have opened by itself, some *thing* had caused this to happen.

Ever so slowly, I walked toward the hallway, with my gun secured. Whatever was opening the door would not be stopped by bullets. The door was, of course, closed and securely latched. I stood in the hallway for awhile, carefully listening and watching for signs of movement. Nothing happened.

Completing the report was the last thing on my mind, but I decided to finish the task. All was quiet as I returned to my desk. I sat stiffly in the chair, determined not to be chased from the building. Minutes ticked by as I waited for the next occurrence. *All right,* I thought, *if some sort of supernatural phenomenon is going on here, it will have to deal with me. I will not be run off by some annoying spirit held over from the Klondike era. Not Alan White, no sir!*

You might say my sitting and listening while encamped behind the desk was admirable; after awhile, though, it became boring. I was about to write the whole episode off to midnight shifts, when the door screeched shut. Once again, I got the familiar feeling of hair leaping to attention on my neck; however not as bad this time.

Is that the best you can do? I smugly thought. *What's to closing a door? Any old spirit can handle that, you two-bit piece of suspended animation!* As I considered additional insults, a two-bit something began to walk across the creaky wooden floor of the museum above me. I was familiar with the sound. I thought this new noise might be a result of my over-active imagination, but the footsteps were, well, *hauntingly real.*

When my heartbeat slowed to a reasonable level, I studied the new sound. Definite footsteps could be heard crossing the floor from east to west. They would stop for a time, and then return to where they had begun. Having no intention of going up to the museum, I chose to remain at my desk, in a cold sweat.

The door screeched again. I threw up my hands in disgust. *Great, this is all I need! Everyone thought I was nuts for coming to Alaska in the first place, and now I find myself in a haunted department.* I sat in my chair for another half hour, listening to the supernatural activities. Then anger set in. *I didn't need this. What had I done to deserve this phenomenon?* I was now totally disgusted.

The door shut again. I jumped from my chair, just as whatever was walking around upstairs bumped into something. I began my first attempt at ghost-busting. "Now, knock it off!" I yelled as loudly as I could. The sound of my voice startled me and, apparently, the spirits moving about. There was absolute silence. *Ha! They're intimidated by me!* I thought.

Then continuing my tirade, I strutted around the room. "I did not travel over three thousand miles to be haunted! Why don't you guys, or girls, or whatever, find some other building to run amuck in? Hey you, upstairs! You bump into something? Good! I hope you stubbed your, ah … thing! Now, go back to wherever you go during the day and leave me alone! You're really starting to tick me off!"

Returning to my chair, I enjoyed the new peace and quiet. My fit seemed to have worked.

Later in my shift, I went back out on patrol, feeling rather good about myself. *Told them a thing or two,* I smugly thought as I drove down Broadway and checked out a few buildings.

Larry relieved me at the shift change, but I said nothing about ghostly wanderings. A bright sunny day had dawned and now it all seemed like a dream. Besides, I wasn't sure I wanted to share an experience like this. I had no idea how common it was for someone who carried a weapon for a living to experience strange night moves.

Luckily, the City Hall spirits left me alone—most of the time. Every few weeks though, the midnight shift would get weird. After listening for awhile, I would yell, "Knock it off!" and all would be quiet for the rest of the night. I became so used to this procedure that I started to be rather matter-of-fact about it.

On one of the few days Larry and I had off together, we were sitting in his living room. "Hey Larry," I asked, "you ever hear anything, you know, *strange*, working in the office late at night?"

The look on his face was telling. "What do you mean when you say *strange*?" Larry asked, choosing his words carefully.

"Ah, you know, doors closing, footsteps overhead in the museum, that sort of thing."

"Oh, thank you," Larry sighed. "I thought I was going insane or something."

Larry and I discussed the situation for some time. "Just yell 'Knock it off!'" I said, feeling like an old pro. "They hate that."

Excerpt from the book *Alaska Behind Blue Eyes* by Alan L. White. For more information, visit www.alanlwhite.com.

Her Voice

When I first heard the woman's voice, I had been involved in the thirty-five-year-old investigation for eight years. This particular cold case involved the murder of a twenty-three-year-old college student in 1969. Like so many others, this one had been shelved time after time over the years due to a lack of investigative leads. It was the kind of case that every police department has—the one referred to as *the case*—and everyone knows which one you are talking about.

Finally, after years of dead-ends, science might come to our rescue. Breakthrough DNA-extraction technology had just become available and evidence from the case had been delivered to the lab for analysis. There was nothing left for us to do at this point but to wait patiently for the results. We desperately hoped for a break in the case.

During this time I traveled to Baton Rouge, Louisiana, to attend an FBI-sponsored violent crimes seminar. While there, I spoke to several of my counterparts at length, explaining what our scientists were attempting to do with the evidence while fishing for any investigative ideas they might have.

After many hours of exchanging tall-tales and war stories, I found myself back in my hotel room in the early morning hours and quickly fell asleep—or so I thought. After what seemed like only minutes, I distinctly heard a female voice softly calling my name. As I hovered in that familiar valley between sleep and conscious thought, the voice continued to slowly call my name: "Eric, wake up. I need you." The voice seemed to be getting closer, increasing in volume and clarity, until I knew I was fully awake. As I lay there, trying to understand what I thought was a strange dream, I once again heard her voice urgently calling my name and telling me to wake up. I was needed.

The voice was so clear and so close—it was right next to me! I could feel her breath on my neck! This realization startled me and I instantly jumped out of bed and fumbled for the light switch. Maybe someone was playing a trick on me and was hiding in the room. Upon turning on the lights I saw no one. I searched the entire room, including the closet, bathroom, and behind the TV. I even opened the door to check the hallway for stragglers—all to no avail. I was alone.

Needless to say it took me quite awhile to fall asleep after this scare. Eventually I chalked it up to being a bad dream from sleeping in a strange bed . . . until I returned home.

On the following Monday, as I sat in a meeting sipping coffee and listening half-heartedly to the speaker, I received a 911 page from the lab. Could this be what we've been waiting for all these years? I excused myself from the room and immediately called the lab. They had a positive CODIS notification! Score one for the scientists! They had done what no one else had—identify the person responsible for this crime.

By analyzing the DNA that was embedded into the weave of the victim's clothing by the offender, and matching that DNA profile to a list of known felons, the lab was able to give us a name. We could now move the investigation forward and bring it to a successful conclusion.

Although I have never believed in ghosts or the paranormal, I am unable to provide any earthly explanation for what I experienced in that hotel room. I believe it was the victim calling to me and telling me I was needed. Her message of "Eric, wake up—I need you" is etched firmly in my mind. I can still hear her voice and feel her breath on my neck. She knew it was time for me to wake up; that things were happening that needed my attention.

She was right.

Wake Up!

About five or six years ago, I was driving home alone, towards Adrian, Michigan. It was close to midnight and I was tired after working the afternoon shift. I was driving about sixty-five miles an hour along a highway with farming fields on both sides when I fell asleep at the wheel of my small pick-up truck.

Just as my vehicle hit the gravel on the shoulder, I heard a loud voice shouting, "WAKE UP! WAKE UP!" I opened my eyes and realized I was headed straight for the north shoulder of the road. My head was tilted forward; I knew I had been sound asleep.

Awake now, I looked toward the passenger seat and saw a man sitting there. He was staring me in the face, leaning toward me, and yelling at me to wake up. I could only see his outline because a bright glow seemed to come from within and around him. We were looking at each other eye-to-eye; but the brightness was so great, I could only see the contours of his face and body. I'll never forget his intent stare.

I immediately looked forward and realized I was approaching the top edge of the ditch. I didn't panic. I took my foot off the gas and steered back towards the roadway. Once I had the truck under control, I looked toward my passenger—but no one was there. A dim light was still glowing, but it soon faded away.

It was not a dream. I saw a man, and I felt his presence in my truck. This is an experience I will never forget. If I had driven off the roadway at the speed I was going, chances are my truck would have flipped and death or serious injury would have been the consequence.

I truly believe a guardian angel saved my life that night.

The Bower's Harbor Inn

My partner and I were working the midnight shift. It was a cloudy, windy night. He was telling me about an encounter that he and another officer had with our local haunted restaurant, the Bower's Harbor Inn. The fact that we were driving on a stretch of road on a peninsula that was directly across from the restaurant reminded him of the story.

In the middle of his monologue, Central Dispatch called for available units to respond to an alarm—at the Bower's Harbor Inn! Of course, we were the closest unit, so we responded.

When we arrived at the restaurant, my partner went around one side of the building and I went around the other. I noticed a stairway leading up to a door on the second floor. I climbed the stairs to check the door. When I turned the handle, the door opened. I gently pulled the door closed so that it rested on the casing—but it wasn't completely shut. I notified my partner that I had discovered an open door.

When the key holder arrived, he let us into the building. My partner and I cleared the first floor of the restaurant and then proceeded to the second floor. When we reached the door I had left open, it was completely shut and *locked!* In order to open the door again, we had to use the key.

There was nobody in the building.

This Time, I Was the Victim

It was the beginning of the 2003 holiday season when my wife and I were invited to a holiday fundraiser at a posh restaurant in Detroit's Indian Village area. The purpose was to raise money for less fortunate inner-city kids so they could be supplied with shoes for the upcoming winter.

I did my homework on the event. The mayor and some federal judges were also invited, so I trusted that their security details would have things well in hand. Thus, I did not fear for my wife's and my safety or that of the other guests, including a police lieutenant from my department and his wife.

The entertainment, food, and drinks were fantastic. A very nice evening, even though the mayor never showed nor did any of the federal judges or other celebrities as promised.

Things were winding down for the evening. The valet girl found me and gave me the keys to my vehicle, saying she was going off duty and would no longer be responsible for my truck. Then, she ran out the door. I went to the door to look for my truck, saw it, and was returning to the restaurant when two gunmen broke in, rushed me with a gun pointed directly at my face, grabbed me by the necktie, and forced me into the dining room. One of them fired a shot next to my head and announced the hold-up. I went to the ground and a second shot was fired, fragmenting when it hit a $40,000 grand piano. A fragment of the slug struck a lady.

I was not armed, as I believed the mayor's security detail would be present. It's a good thing I wasn't because if my weapon were seen I am positive I would have become another Detroit homicide statistic.

I believed I was going to be shot in the head as I lay face down on the floor. I threw my cash on the floor, as the gunman demanded everybody's wallets. My wallet had a badge and police ID in it. If that were revealed, I most assuredly would have been shot.

For some unknown reason, I envisioned a crime scene photo with me lying face down on the floor with my brains spilling out of my skull. I was not about to allow that to happen. My wife was only a few feet away, hiding underneath a table. She appeared to be okay.

I began to pray, and I felt the presence of a guardian angel. The fear left me and I was able to focus on the criminals' actions so that I might become the best witness and see them led off to prison in handcuffs.

I threw my wallet under a table and it landed face open with the badge in full sight. I flipped it closed. How they never saw this had to be the work of an angel.

I was kicked in the groin as the number two gunman gathered up the cash and wallets. They went to a second dining room and I heard screaming and another gunshot. Then all was silent. I immediately called 911 to report the armed robbery with shots fired. I was still on the phone when the first patrol officer arrived, calming everyone and checking for injuries. Before I knew it, there were uniformed officers all over.

Suspects were being picked up in the neighborhood and brought back to the scene, but I couldn't identify any of them. My wife and I were thankful to go home alive that night with only relatively minor injuries.

About a week later, we were sitting in our kitchen having our Saturday morning coffee, watching the local Detroit news program when I saw a story about a major arrest having been made by the Violent Crimes Task Force, a team comprised of FBI Agents, Michigan State Police Troopers, Detroit Police Officers, and some suburban Detroit officers. The number one gunman's mug shot was displayed and I immediately recognized him as the one responsible for the armed robbery where we were victims.

All weekend I telephoned the investigator assigned to our case, with no reply. Monday morning, I was able to contact a member of the Task Force and told him our story. The bad guy had been arrested with four others responsible for murder, armed robberies, and carjacking. A fifth suspect, a juvenile, had fled to Alabama, and the FBI was after him. Their specialty was robbing patrons at fundraisers.

Weeks later, I was able to pick him out in a line-up at the Wayne County Jail. Although I never saw the case go to trial, as the number one suspect had already been convicted of first degree murder and sentenced to life without parole, I believe it was the intervention of an angel that saved my life that night. And also some Divine Intervention that led me to watch the local news channel and see the scumbag's mug shot.

Ghost Alarm

Some police officers can never turn off their "light switch," even while on vacation. They always notice peculiar things!

In 1997, my wife and I rented an old one-bedroom cottage for a month on the island of Boca Grande, which lies on the Gulf Coast north of Ft. Myers. My wife had written to the Chamber of Commerce on the island and learned about this cottage. The owner was contacted, and she explained that at one time it had been a fisherman's cottage and later the caretaker's cottage for a much larger home next door. The name of the cottage was *Journey's End*.

When we arrived, the lessor greeted us and entertained us with some of the local lore. One story she told was of a murder that had occurred either in the cottage we rented or in the large house next door. I do not remember which, but it was rumored both of the houses were haunted.

The cottage was old but clean and the view of the Gulf was magnificent. We saw dolphins in the water in front of the cottage each morning. It was exactly the type of vacation we wanted.

After we had been there about a week, my wife and I went to bed one evening about eleven o'clock. Shortly after turning out the lights, the fire alarm above our bed rang very loudly! We nearly jumped out of our skins. It continued for a significant period of time, perhaps thirty seconds, then quit.

I quickly turned on the lights and looked for smoke. There was none. My wife and I are nonsmokers. I checked the house thoroughly for some sign of smoke or combustion, but there was none. I then decided to remove the battery so that the alarm would not sound again, as the noise was deafening.

I got a chair and stood on it to reach the alarm. When I opened the cover, I discovered there was no battery in the alarm! My wife also confirmed the fact that the alarm had no battery.

Did residual power cause the alarm to ring? We had been in the cottage for a week without the alarm sounding. Any residual current would have been dissipated. The alarm was connected to no other power source. There was no combustion or smoke present. It was the simple type of circular alarm with plastic housing that operated from a 9-volt battery. It never sounded again during our stay.

How could this have happened?

The Trooper's Riddle

by Tom Brosman

Shannon was a trooper with just a few years on.
It was a job that suited her and she worked from dusk til dawn.
One night a Camaro flew by at 90-plus
Shannon lit it up and took after the car in a rush.

Dispatch had ran the plates by the time she rolled the Camaro over
And walked up beside the car that was parked alongside the shoulder.
A teenaged girl behind the wheel was cussing and throwing a fit.
"My dad is a senator, just so you know. Now give me a warning and git!

He has a lot of influence all across this state
And if you let me off, I'll tell him you cut me a break."
The trooper kept her cool and wrote a modest citation
The violator's expression as she signed was a battle declaration.

Three weeks later on a July day, Shannon's sergeant called her in.
"There has been a serious charge placed against you by a senator about his
    kid.
The papers I am serving you say you yelled and cussed at his girl
And that you called her the "B" word twice and other insults hurled."

Eventually, the charges were dropped, but they took their toll on Shannon.
She lost a lot of sleep and felt betrayed, like she was shot at from a cannon.
Finally, she kind of got over it and summer passed, then fall
Christmas was just up ahead, her favorite time of all.

She had to work on Christmas day, but her dad always made dinner.
She had popped a couple of DUIs by noon and warned a passing speeder.
The afternoon went slowly, with few vehicles rolling by.
At three p.m. dispatch sent her to a wreck where the RP thought the girl
    driving had died.

It was lights and siren to the blind curve on a knoll
Where the driver of a Camaro had sheered off a power pole.
The driver inside the crumpled car groaned faintly through the broken glass
And blood in gouts was flowing from a deep arterial gash.

"I need an aid car with some blood and call the PUD.
I've got to help the victim now before she bleeds out in front of me."
The trooper applied pressure at the point to make the bleeding stem
And she thought it was so ironic that she had saved the driver again.

She signed out of service at her house, working an hour over
And she took off her bloody uniform and stood underneath a good warm
    shower.
She called her dad to tell him she'd not be there til a quarter til.
Her dad met her at his door and hugged his darling girl.

He had made a table full of food and had a tree that glistened.
Oh, he had been a trooper, too, and knew there was a time to listen.
Her mother had been like that, too, had that cloudy look when a storm was
    brewing.
He made small talk as they ate, of fruit trees, weather, and BBQing

He looked across the table to everything he held dear
"Care to tell your dad what caused those wiped away tears?"
She should have known that her dad, who'd been a troop for thirty years,
Could sense her mood a block away with instinct heeded, needed over the
    years.

She glanced around the table at the ham and salad and pie
But her father's favorite food was from his fruit trees he'd canned and put by.
He had been so lost when her mother died, with a daughter and a house
    and the patrol.
But he pulled it off to get her raised and she loved him for it all.

"Well … it's a riddle, Daddy, really and one that I can't solve.
I work so hard to protect and serve with all of my resolve.
I cited a speeder way last summer and she accused me of close to crimes
I was cleared after a month of sleeplessness and a fair amount of crying.

"Today, I saved that speeder's life in a wreck that she had caused.
There is no doubt in my mind I won't get any thanks or applause.
Where's the justice in a system when troopers risk their lives
Only to be wrongly accused, like the slice from betrayer's knives?

"How did you deal with a system for over thirty years
When the very person that you rescued could give you grief and fears?"
The father chuckled to his daughter, which was not what she had asked
He dished some homegrown fruit for her and filled her empty glass.

"Daughter, try the prunes, I picked the plums and canned them in sweet juices."
The young trooper humored the older one, knowing that hurry was useless.
She placed the pits on the edge of her plate and the juicy pulp she enjoyed
Until, at last, the man was ready to hand down a tool that he had employed.

He, too, had been in spots before when the helped citizen helped himself to the trooper.
It had taken him years of pressure and frustration to find a way that was smoother.
But he had found some peace with a system that had brought him consternation.
"When you went to Shelton, I knew that someday we would have this conversation.

"If you allow it, the trooper's life can fuel resentment and frustration.
Consider the prune pits on your plate, my daughter, and learn a valuable lesson.
Unless you are suicidal, you don't eat the prune with the pit.
There is a downside to carrying a badge and you are up against it.

"Some of those you try to help will take a swipe at the blue shirt as you wear it.
The answer to your riddle is that you can't have fruit without the pit.
Don't try to swallow the fruit whole and don't let bitterness build up in your soul.
Or the pit will choke you and bitterness will make you old."

"Vision is the art of seeing things invisible."

Jonathan Swift

Dreams & Intuition

Innovations in science and technology have been inspired by dreams and intuition, yet our culture oftentimes dismisses these avenues as legitimate ways for pursuing research or investigation. Receiving insights in these extraordinary ways can be a source of survival—our intuitive intelligence is capable of interacting with facts and situations that go beyond what is available through our five senses. In our line of work, we utilize anything to save lives.

"The intellect has little to do on the road to discovery. There comes a leap in consciousness, call it Intuition or what you will, the solution comes to you and you don't know how or why."

Albert Einstein

The Fatal Vortex

It seems like only yesterday when I was sent to a house alarm call that could have resulted in fatalities. Typically most calls are false alarms. Whether the wind blows open a shutter or a resident accidentally sets off the alarm—usually house alarms are harmless. I believe that only by Divine grace am I alive today to share this story . . .

I pull into the driveway at the same time the key holder arrives. The key holder is the person an alarm company calls when a house alarm goes off. In this case, it is the homeowner's thirty-year-old son.

I tell the man to stay by his car until I secure the area. He says, "I know my mother is home and everything's cool, but I don't know what is going on."

I check the doors, windows, and garage entranceway for any possible forced entry, but everything looks secure. I say, "Go ahead and open the garage door." I remind him to stay by his car while I check the inside of the house.

I enter the dimly lit garage and walk to the door that leads into the house. I knock on the door and announce, "State Police!" and push open the door.

At that moment, a white-haired elderly woman steps out of nowhere and slowly points a .20 gauge shotgun directly in my face!

Even though I have turned on the garage light, she doesn't seem to notice I am a uniformed trooper. In my attempt to escape the "fatal vortex" and un-holster my weapon, I stumble backward but do not fall. The fatal vortex is that hypothetical space we're taught about in school; that space shaped like a funnel that you never want to be caught in.

I was definitely at the tip of that funnel. I had no safety zone and no spatial advantage.

As I try not to lose my balance, I hear CLICK. The old lady has actually pulled the trigger! Not only does this sound signify my life may instantly be over, but it also means she *means* to shoot!

Somehow I know this woman is the resident and not an intruder. I wonder why I didn't draw my weapon before I stepped into the garage, which is what we are taught to do as a precaution. I am grateful I didn't because I might have shot her if my gun had been in my hand. I yell at her repeatedly, "I'm a police officer! I'm a police officer! *Don't shoot! Look at my uniform! I'm a police officer!*"

The woman's son starts yelling at her, too. Who knows what this woman is thinking? How can she not see my uniform? It takes both of us to convince her I am the police and not there to hurt her. It is a miracle she does not kill me.

After I settled her down, I asked, "What were you thinking? Didn't you hear me knocking at the door? Didn't you hear me say 'state police'? Why didn't you call 911? They would have told you who was knocking! When you press the panic button for the alarm, police are *supposed* to come and help you, *right?*" (According to the alarm company, she had pressed the panic button.)

As I'm scolding her and trying to regain my composure, I open the double-barrel action to make the weapon safe. Out pops a shotgun shell! I can see that shell moving in slow motion . . . jumping out of the chamber into the air . . . spiraling . . . twirling . . . dancing . . . and then finally hitting the floor with a THUNK and rolling to its final resting place between my two feet. I didn't have to pick it up to know it was a heavy *unspent* round and that by the grace of God the gun hadn't fired.

It humbled me to realize how close I had come to death. And, to make matters worse, I found out she was the widow of a state trooper. I could have killed a fellow trooper's wife!

I shot the gun outdoors. There was nothing wrong with it! The woman pulled the trigger—I should have been killed.

There are some things that have happened to me in this job that I just don't talk about. This is one of them. I don't know why I didn't shoot that woman, especially after she pulled the trigger. How did I know she was really a "good guy?" Whatever you want to call it—intuition, a sixth sense, or an angel—I depended on it—and we are both alive.

A Special Spot

Worried parents reported that their sixteen-year-old son was missing. They thought he had run away, but they had no idea where. When I arrived at their home, something didn't feel right. I asked the parents more questions than usual. I asked if the boy got good grades in school and if he had any troubles he was dealing with. They said his grades had gone down recently and that he was on anti-depressants.

When the parents mentioned anti-depressants, I got a very clear thought: *This is not a runaway complaint.* I don't know why the word *anti-depressant* triggered this thought, because usually it doesn't mean anything to me. I know that anti-depressants are often very helpful to people, even children.

I looked in the boy's bedroom and saw two unopened packs of cigarettes by his bed. I thought, *What sixteen-year-old boy leaves two packs of cigarettes behind?* Most teenagers carry their cigarettes with them, especially if their parents allow them to smoke. This was the second hint that the incident was not what it appeared to be.

I didn't want to ask, but I did: "Do you have any weapons in the house?" The father said yes and that he had already looked. All of the cases were present. I asked if he had opened the cases, and he said no. I told him to go check. When he returned, he reported that a rifle, a Ruegar .280, was missing. I suddenly knew their son was probably dead, but I didn't say anything. Not yet. It was the third clear thought that came through my mind.

I got the urge to take a look outside. Sure enough, I found footwear impressions in the snow that appeared to be the boy's— and they seemed to lead into the woods.

The snow was patchy this time of year, so I called Dispatch for canine assistance. While I waited for the dog and handler to arrive, I telephoned the boy's best friend. I asked if there were any special spots where the boy might have walked. I knew most teenagers have one. Because the snow was minimal, I knew that even with a dog, it might be difficult to track the boy unless I had an idea where to head. Sure enough, the boy had a special spot.

When the canine officer arrived, the dog picked up a scent. It was an overcast winter day. The canine handler, the dog, and I followed the boy's scent toward his special spot. I was glad I had called the boy's best friend for directions so that I knew we were on the right track. As we walked I realized how breathtaking this area is. The near-pristine woodlands, hilly terrain, and sand dunes of Leelanau County, Michigan, are absolutely gorgeous. The smell of the pines was pungent and pure. *What a pity this young man has taken his own life, when there is so much to love about this land and life.* I already knew we'd find him dead.

We continued to follow the boy's scent. The trees opened up into a small open area in the woods. This was his special spot. We saw him. He had shot his head off with the missing rifle. I was so thankful I had trusted my intuition and hadn't allowed the boy's parents to come with us. The bloody scene was too gory for any parent ever to see.

Although it was hard and their grief unbearable, the boy's parents were relieved I had found their son.

I thought about this case several times afterward. If I had treated this situation like a routine runaway complaint, the boy's body might never have been found. Corpses are often eaten by animals—sometimes without a trace left—especially in this area of Northern Michigan known for its vultures, eagles, and coyotes. I am sure many of my fellow comrades also rely on intuitive thoughts. Most of us seldom, if ever, talk about it, of course. Policemen are expected to rely on logic and "just the facts."

The Skull in the River

As a forensic artist and road patrol trooper for the State Police, I have worked on many interesting cases. Little did I know that a cardboard box placed on my desk one sweltering August day would contain one of the most challenging and emotional cases of my career. A year earlier I had completed a facial reconstruction course at the FBI Academy in Quantico.

The box contained a human skull and was my second skeletal case. The first case I worked on was still unsolved—the charred body of a black female was still at the morgue, waiting to be identified. This new case held little more promise. It had already sat on a property room shelf for nine years.

As I leafed through the police reports, I learned that the skull had been dredged out of the Clinton River, which runs through Mt. Clemens, Michigan, in 1992. A construction worker on a bulldozer thought he had found the "biggest mushroom he had ever seen." When he jumped off the earthmover to kick it from its position in the soggy marsh, he was shocked to discover it was actually a human cranium. The rest of the body, including the lower jaw, was never recovered.

Although missing person reports were carefully checked, the skull remained unidentified and was packed away in a property room at the sheriff's office. In the summer of 2003, the property room was cleaned out and the skull was sent to a Michigan State Police crime lab for possible DNA and comparison purposes. One of the senior members at the lab suggested it be sent to a forensic artist to do a reconstruction. Several weeks later, the skull was placed on my desk.

First I took it to the Michigan State University Anthropology

Lab, where I asked the anthropologist to examine it and give me a biological profile of who the person I would be reconstructing. He told me it belonged to a Caucasian male, between the ages of eighteen and thirty. Since I wanted to do a three-dimensional reconstruction with clay, the missing mandible posed a huge problem. The lab was nice enough to let me borrow a specimen from a body that had been donated.

I fished through several boxes of bones in the lab labeled "Caucasian males" before finding one with a similar bite pattern. With my borrowed jawbone and several x-rays of the seven teeth that were left in the cranium, I took the skull back to my post to start work.

For the next eight months, I juggled the reconstruction in between normal working duties. As the face began to emerge, I began to get a feeling about what this man must have looked like. For instance, I could see that his teeth had been extremely well cared for. He could afford a dentist and he took good care of himself. From this I assumed his socio-economic place in life.

I also surmised that he was good looking. Since the skull was dredged out of the river in 1992, I figured he must have been in the water for some time to become completely disarticulated and skeletal. Therefore, I guessed his hairstyle would be from the late 1980s or early 1990s. I decided to sculpt a longer, falling-behind-the-ears hairstyle, in brown, since that is the dominant hair color of the Caucasian race. I also gave him brown eyes—both an intuitive and practical guess. I reminded myself that a reconstruction doesn't have to look *exactly* like the person—but there has to be something about it that triggers a sense of recognition in just one person who sees it and thinks, *Hmmm, that might be so-and-so.*

Finally in April 2004, the reconstruction was ready to be released to the media. I held a press conference and was shocked to find that almost every media source in the metropolitan-

Detroit area showed up to get the story. The following days were filled with newscasts, phone calls, and interviews.

About a week later, a District Sergeant who worked as an accident re-constructionist in my district phoned me. He had seen a photo of my reconstruction in the *Detroit Free Press* and it reminded him of a young guy who had gone missing from the Algonac area when he was a road patrol officer there. He said the guy's name was Shawn Raymond.

Since this was my first real tip, I didn't have any particular feeling or hope that this was going to go anywhere. I went to the Clay Township Police Department and asked if I could see the Shawn Raymond case. The officers were all too familiar with the case. Shawn's file revealed that his mother had reported him missing after he was not seen for two days. Shawn was nineteen at the time and a recent graduate of Algonac High School. There were several photos of Shawn in the file, including one of his high school yearbook photos. I noticed he was an incredibly good looking guy, with feather-brown hair and a glowing white smile—just like I had imagined.

I didn't immediately see a resemblance between the clay sculpture and Shawn, though I did notice Shawn's dental charts. There was crucial information on these charts. The skull and Shawn had the same two bicuspids removed for orthodontic purposes. This was a clue I could not ignore. I immediately took the case back to my post and began calling to locate Shawn's dentist to get x-rays for comparison.

The first dentist led me to a dead end, literally. His wife sorrowfully informed me that her husband's practice had closed after his death and she had destroyed all the remaining records, including the x-rays. My stomach lurched. I thought, *Is this the end of my investigation?*

I feverishly pressed the keys on my telephone to call Shawn's orthodontist. Amazingly, he was still practicing in the area. And, yes, he still had Shawn's file, which included panoramic x-rays of Shawn's teeth. I picked them up a day later.

I was ready to put my anthropology degree to the test and compare the dental films. As I drove the x-rays back to the post, I phoned my dad, who has thirty years experience as a trooper, detective, and forensic artist. I chatted with him nervously, telling him, "It's got to be him. There are so many coincidences!"

My dad urged me to be calm. "Now, settle down. This is only your first tip," he said.

Back at the post, I scotch-taped the bite-wing x-rays I had taken at MSU to my office window and then, with hands shaking, taped the panoramic film from Shawn's orthodontist file underneath it. Undeniably, even to my little-trained eyes . . . it was a match! Now all I needed was the final okay from an ontologist—a forensic dentist. I sought one out in the area and made an appointment to meet with him at his office the following day.

Morning seemed like it would never come. I had several conversations with my dad, who continued to tell me, "Don't get your hopes up too high." But I was beyond help. In my mind, I knew it had to be Shawn. There was nothing that was going to convince me otherwise (except, maybe, this expert I was about to meet).

As I drove to his office, I tried to calm myself down. I had thoughts like, *What if it isn't him? What if I have to start all over again?* My stomach was in complete knots. A soft rain was falling as I approached the parking lot and turned in. I made one last call to dad and told him, "I'll phone you with the answer as soon as I'm out!"

When I met the dentist, I sized him up to be on his last year or two before retirement. He was elderly. He had me set the reconstruction on a stool and took his own panoramic films of the skull through the clay. I guess he didn't like the bite wings

I brought with me as proof. When his x-rays were developed, he held up Shawn's films and the freshly taken films to the fluorescent lighting above him. He nonchalantly said, "Nope, that's not him."

I was dumbfounded. My heart sank. I fought off tears and began to tremble. Here I was, in my professionally tailored uniform, holding a human skull encased in twenty-five pounds of clay, and I was fighting to choke back tears. I mumbled to him, softly at first, "No, you're wrong . . ."

As my vision cleared and I regained my composure, I took a quick glance at the films he still held in his hands. Still fighting tears of disappointment, I stated clearly and louder, without reservation, "No, you're WRONG!" I snatched the films from his hand. He had been holding one of the films *backward*! I handed them back to him the correct way. He raised the films toward the lights again and—without hesitation—said, "Yup, that's him!"

The trip from his room to my car seemed like I was running in slow motion. Once I was in my car, I dialed my phone. "Dad, it's him!" And, for the next half-hour, I sobbed. At least my tears were of joy and not sorrow. I was so glad that Shawn was found, and I was thankful that his family would find out that he was no longer missing, that his remains had indeed been identified.

Note: Facial reconstruction requires both scientific and intuitive work to successfully identify someone. Features such as the nose, lips, style of hair, etc., are almost strictly intuitive guesses.

Breaking the Rules

While on patrol, an oncoming vehicle sped by me at almost 100 miles per hour. I had a feeling that something was wrong, that this wasn't just a speeder gone wild. I made a U-turn and promptly stopped the vehicle. A man jumped out of the driver's seat and frantically ran toward me. He cried desperately, "My son has been stung by a bee and he's *dying*! Can you help us, please? He's in back of my car. He can't breathe!" I saw the boy's head resting on his mother's lap; he was gasping for air.

The couple did not realize that the hospital they were heading for had recently closed its doors. Even though I was a fairly new trooper and still conditioned to following protocol, I decided to use my God-given power of discretion. There wasn't any time to wait. I piled both parents and their son in the backseat of my patrol car and headed for the nearest hospital.

I drove faster than I'd ever driven before—even faster than in Recruit School. The boy was suffocating. It was obvious his throat was swelled up. And he appeared to be losing consciousness.

Boisterous from adrenaline, I said to the boy, "Hey, look! All the cars are pulling over for you! Wow, they see our lights and sirens! How do you like being in a patrol car and riding so fast? We'll be at the hospital in no time, sweetheart."

I was probably more excited than his parents. I don't know how I kept my voice from cracking. I kept urging the parents to keep him awake. I was so scared for the boy.

It was summertime and traffic was bumper-to-bumper with all of the tourists in town. As I wove safely between the vehicles I thought divine intervention must be at hand. We didn't encounter any backups or typical delays.

Other thoughts rushed through my head, though, like *Will I be reprimanded or fired for this?* I knew calling an ambulance would have taken too long, but I was breaking departmental rules. I considered pending lawsuits. I finally shut out those thoughts and silently affirmed, *I don't care if I'm written up. They can fire me, if they want. The boy is hurt. I know I'm doing the right thing by following my instinct.*

We arrived at the hospital in less than ten minutes, and the boy was rushed to emergency care. The parents thanked me repeatedly, and then I left. I returned to my daily business, though I wasn't looking forward to seeing my desk sergeant. I was certain I would be confronted.

Later that day, when I returned to the Post, I was surprised to learn that the boy's parents had stopped by to thank me again. Fellow troopers greeted me with smiles and the desk sergeant actually patted me on the back and said, "Kudos, kiddo. Good job, but get back to work." At the end of my shift I went home and thought the incident was forgotten.

When I turned on the eleven o'clock news, however, I saw the boy's attending physician talking with a news reporter. I thought to myself, *Wow, this made the news?* and I turned up the volume on the television.

The doctor said, ". . . by far the worst case of anaphylactic shock I have ever treated. If that trooper hadn't brought the boy here so quickly, or had waited even five more minutes, this boy would not have survived."

I chuckled and thought, *Well, that's cool. I hope my boss is watching this, because everything I did was against the rules!* Then I shut off the TV and went to bed.

I was content. Divine guidance had directed me—and the boy was alive and well.

Since I had broken departmental rules, I was disqualified for any life-saving award. But, one month later, I received a letter of appreciation from the governor himself! I laughed. The parents were so appreciative they had called the governor. I framed it and hung it on my wall. To this day it reminds me that no badge or trophy can ever bring me the same joy as knowing those parents brought their boy home safely. Any material award would now be a total insult.

The Bone Lady

We are called to a drowning. A snowmobile with two riders has gone through the ice. We dive in and find the snowmobile but no bodies. The sheriff contacts Sandra Anderson, a famous woman known for finding bones and bodies in water. This is my first contact with the Bone Lady.

Sandra brings her dog that can smell dead bodies in the water. She says her dog can smell the gasses emitted by dead bodies, even in water. After a couple of hours she announces, "The dog is indicating the bodies are not out there."

"How can you tell?" I ask.

She says, "Well, I can tell by the way the dog acts."

A week later one of the bodies shows up—only about 150 feet from where we were searching. This is my first red flag that something is wrong with the Bone Lady.

My next contact with her is in regards to a woman, Cherita Thomas, who had been missing since 1980. We believe she is a homicide victim.

Detective McGregor and Dave Marthaler (FBI) take Sandra in the woods to search for Cherita's remains. The first time they search the woods, nothing is found. They take Sandra to the same area a second time, and they start finding bones. I photograph the bones and e-mail the photos to a forensic anthropologist. He says they are animal bones.

I recall Sandra telling me that her dog would *never* hit on animal bones. Another red flag is raised.

I start to get bad vibes about the Bone Lady. She always wants to *return* to a site . . . she never finds bones the first time, only on the second or third visit. And, these are areas that have already been thoroughly checked.

By this time, the crime team has discussed other missing people with Sandra. We have provided all kinds of information to her, and she continues to return to the same areas where she's already been.

Miraculously, we start to find human bones. We even bring in the FBI Recovery Team on one of the searches.

We are on a suspected location and the dog is marking areas. To indicate the location of a bone, the dog puts its nose to the ground and then lies down. Sandra sticks a flag in the ground wherever the dog does this. We start searching the flagged areas. Several of us are down on our knees in one area, when the Bone Lady says, "The dog is indicating there is a bone over there."

"Where? Where is he indicating?" I ask.

She says, "Over there. Right where he's at . . ."

I look again. "We've already looked over there. There's nothing there. Where do you mean?"

And she says, "Right there. The dog is sitting on it."

"How can you tell the dog is sitting on a bone?!"

"I can just tell. He's sitting on it. Reach underneath and grab the bone!"

I thought, *Yeah, right. I'm going to reach under the dog and find a bone . . . this is a joke!*

She sees the look on my face and says, "I'm serious!" She moves the dog up and low and behold, the dog was sitting on a bone!

The anthropologist on the scene determines it is a finger bone. "Yeah, it's definitely human," he says. Then he sticks it up to his nose and says, "Smell this."

I look at him incredulously as I think, *Right, the dog's ass was just on it and now you want me to smell this bone . . .*

He says, "Seriously, tell me what it smells like."

I put it under my nose and sniff. "Smells like chlorine bleach."

"I was thinking more like ammonia, but yeah, bleach or ammonia," he says.

"Why would this bone smell like ammonia or bleach after all these years?" I ask.

We discuss the possibilities. The best reason we can surmise is that the murderer poured chlorine bleach or ammonia on the body when it was decomposing to get rid of the smell. We search further and find more human bones.

Meanwhile, we are still searching for Cherita Thomas. John Lucy and Jenny Patchin from the crime lab have joined us. The Bone Lady is here too. On one of our previous searches, Sandra was told about two hunters in a white Ford Bronco who have been missing since 1969. Well, she confused Oscoda County where that case happened with Oscoda, Michigan, which is far away in Iosco County. One of the finger bones she discovered on this search was wrapped in camouflage material—as if there was still flesh on it. It seemed to me as if Sandra was finding evidence for every crime we told her about in this one area, like it was a mass dumping ground for bodies in Iosco County.

Anyway, everybody on the team believes the bones Sandra finds are real. They are excited about the discoveries; I am getting strong feelings the whole time that something just isn't right.

Sandra marked areas in a nearby stream a year ago. As we are walking along, the dog hits on something in the stream. Sandra sticks flags in the water and says, "Let's come back to this. Let's go search another area first, then we'll come back here."

"Whatever," I say, although I think it is odd.

We follow Sandra and the dog to some other areas. She wants to look at what she calls coyote dens. She thinks coyotes drag body bones to their dens. In the bank of the streams where muskrats live—that is what she thinks is a coyote den.

Underneath a stump someone finds a broken bone. Everybody gets excited, "Hey, man, look we found an arm bone!" The anthropologist confirms it is an arm bone.

Sandra then announces, "Well, I'm going to go back down to

the creek." She meant where she had earlier planted the flags in the water. Realize, John, Jenny, Sergeant McGregor, and myself have already sifted this area with screens—right down to the hard bottom of the stream. They removed the muck, etc. and did not find anything.

I decide to accompany Sandra to the stream. She kneels down in the water and says, "It's gotta be right here, gotta be right here. The dog says it's by my foot, dog says it's by my foot . . ." I see her hand go to the back of her leg. "It's gotta be by my foot."

Jokingly, I grab her foot in the water and say, "Hey! I got a WHOLE foot!"

"No, no, seriously," she says, "it's gotta be right down here by my foot." I take my hand off her foot, and sure enough, there is a bone right by her foot.

The bone looks really old and brown. "Oh, you're so good!" she says. "You're always finding bones! Now, let's check this other area where the dogs say there's something." She kneels down in the water and starts searching.

As I watch Sandra in the water, I realize she always wears leg warmers with her boots untied halfway down. There is usually a lot of bulk on top of boots. Sandra says, "It's gotta be right down by my foot, the dog is saying something's here." So I reach in and, sure enough, there's another bone.

"Boy, these things look like they're one hundred years old!" I say.

"Maybe you found an Indian burial ground or something," she suggests.

I'm thinking, *No, this is too coincidental . . . two times in the stream . . . in areas that have already been sifted . . . just her and me . . . no . . . something's wrong . . . it's all just too coincidental.* Of course, I don't say anything. After all, she is famous. She's known worldwide for her work. I don't feel like I know enough yet to question what she is doing, but I do have a *sick* feeling in my head and heart.

47

All of us are at the "coyote den"—the Bone Lady, Dave, Allen, and me. Sandra starts poking a stick in an overturned tree and says, "The dog indicates something's underneath there, something's underneath here. It's gotta be here . . . gotta be right here."

So, I get down on my hands and knees and start crawling into this hole. "Geez," I joke, "I'm going to get my ass bit by some muskrat!"

"Oh no," she says, "the dog says something's there."

The hole is like crawling under a desk. It's a smooth sandy area where the water washed up from the creek. It's all clean sand. There is nothing there. I come out of there laughing. "Hey, there's nothing here."

"Hmm," she says. "Dog is tired, better go. We'll come back tomorrow."

Dave and Allen go back up the bank. I start to follow, then turn around. There's Sandra on her hands and knees, and she says, "My boot came untied . . . hey, I see a bone!"

"What do you mean you see a bone?" I say in disbelief. Of course, everybody turns around and comes back.

She points, "It's right there! I can't reach it though!" The hole is about an arm's length away. I get on my knees and there, where there was nothing before, is a bone sticking out of the sand. I *know* that bone was not there ten minutes ago. Now, I really am sick. I know Sandra is planting bones at this crime scene. I don't know who to talk to about this.

Sandra gives me a hug and says, "You're so good ... you find all these bones!" I think to myself, *Yeah because you just put it there!*

We leave and call it a night. All the other guys are saying, "This is great! We're finding human bones! How exciting!"

I go home thinking, *How am I going to say anything when they're all so excited? She's a famous lady, and I don't have proof—but I know I'm right.* I ask God, "Please, make this easy for me. Please, help me figure this out."

The next morning before we return to the scene, Jenny and John come to me. Jenny says, "Do you think we missed anything when we originally searched that stump and found only beaver chips and stuff like that?"

"Not unless it was something so small you couldn't see it," I answered.

Jenny shook her head. "No, I'm asking do you think we missed anything like this?" She pulls out a piece of fibrous carpet material about two inches by one inch. "Do you think we missed that?"

"NO WAY! No way," I say.

"Sandra went back to the stump and said we missed this." *God has answered my prayers. I am no longer alone in my suspicions.*

"Let me tell you what I think is going on," I say. I tell them all my suspicions and end by saying, "I think she's got to be carrying bones in the back of her pant leg, in her bunched up leg warmers. I think Sandra is actually physically planting the stuff."

We decide we're not letting Sandra out of our sight. One of us will stay with her at all times—no matter what—all day long.

Unfortunately, Sandra manages to walk off with Al and Dave. They are headed to the other coyote dens with the dog. *Damn, now she's out wandering around and none of us are with her!* Sandra "finds" a piece of bone that allegedly has feces on it, which the anthropologist from Michigan State University is able to match with one of the other bones.

Sandra now wants to return to the stream because the dog has alerted her. Jenny says, "I'm going with you." The two of them go off together. Detective McGregor is at the creek too.

Sandy kneels down in the water and starts feeling around. Jenny is watching. She sees Sandy's hand go behind her leg and reach at the back of her boot.

Sandy says, "Oh, I got the bone right here …"

But Jenny grabs Sandy's hand before it can touch the bottom and says, "Yeah, because you just put it there." The two women get into a tug a war over the bone! Sandra tries to throw it back in the water. Imagine that! A bone that she just found—and she wants to throw it in the water?! Well, McGregor is trying to figure out what's going on. He grabs the bone, and that's when Jenny and I tell him, "She's planting the bones."

I was relieved that with the help of God, Jenny and I connected that morning. Otherwise the charade would have lasted much longer.

Eventually, it was found that the bones were from Louisiana State University's medical department. A captain in the fire department, who was training cadaver dogs, was allowed to have the bones and he was supplying them to Sandy. Some of those bones ended up on our scene.

The FBI charged Sandra with ten counts; she pled to five. Some people have appealed their cases based on her finding some of the evidence that convicted them, but the evidence she found was just one small piece to the puzzle in each case. She would "find" the piece that investigators thought they still needed.

Currently, she is lodged in federal prison.

The Tooth Fairy in Reverse

One afternoon I was called to the scene of a pedestrian-vehicle accident at State and Main Streets in Scottville, Michigan. Seven-year-old Christina was crossing the street when she was struck by a man driving a pickup truck. The truck hit her straight-on. She was thrown off her feet before landing on her chin on the concrete.

Luckily, Christina had young, supple bones and escaped with minor injuries. Unfortunately, she lost her front tooth. And it was a new permanent tooth. EMS arrived and took her to the hospital, while at least ten of us remained, police and rescue workers, looking for the little girl's tooth.

Adding to the challenge of finding Christina's tooth on the street was that just prior to the incident, a truck had spilled corn from its dump box while rounding the corner, and thousands of kernels of corn were everywhere. I mean, THOUSANDS!

We searched and searched for at least forty-five minutes—with no luck. Cars would drive over the corn, smashing the kernels, and turn them into all variations of yellow and white. Finally, we had to give up finding the tooth as an impossible feat.

After the last rescue unit pulled away, I drove to my office to finish writing the accident report. As I was sitting at my desk the hospital phoned. I talked to a doctor and he pleaded, "Would you just look one more time for the tooth?"

Although another thirty minutes had gone by, I obediently complied with his request. I truly imagined the tooth was stuck in someone's tire by now, but for some reason, I still saw *possibility*.

Looking for a tooth among thousands of kernels of corn was more frustrating than looking for a needle in a haystack. I finally said to myself, "Okay ... enough of this ... the tooth is still here, it has to be. But, where did it go?" All of a sudden the answer comes to me clearly: *Backtrack the incident again!*

All right, she was hit right here, which caused her to be knocked forward about here ... I carefully pace out the area. I *guess* where Christina landed and hit her chin. Then, I see something in the corn that doesn't look quite right. The color blends in perfectly, but something about it catches my eye. I bend down and look at it closely. Could it be? Yes! It isn't corn. It's *her tooth!*

I was so excited for Christina I hopped into my patrol car and drove to a Shell Mini Mart, grabbed a pint of milk out of the cooler, and dropped the tooth into the milk. My wife, who is a dental assistant, said that is the first thing you do to save a tooth. I yelled to the cashier as I ran out the door, "I'll be back to pay for this later!" Fortunately, she knew me. I raced to the hospital with lights flashing and siren blaring, and ran into the emergency room with the tooth.

The doctor implanted the tooth—and it survived! All I could think of was what a *blessing* to find it! I swear, it was like looking for one bean in a silo of beans—it seemed impossible. Several of us had already looked at that spot several times and couldn't see it. But, when I stopped, tuned in, and didn't try so hard, the tooth was suddenly *there*—in full view.

Christina visits each year, to show me her tooth and her smile. She thanks me every time she sees me. And, yes, I did go back and pay for the milk.

Dream Work

Most of my premonitions and intuitive information manifests while I'm sleeping, although sometimes I receive unusual thoughts consciously.

When I was nineteen years old and living at home, my best friend, Larry, joined the Marine Corps and was sent to Vietnam. Even though he was a couple of years older than me he was a lifetime friend and like a brother to me.

One night, around 2:00 A.M., I thought I heard a loud knock on the door and suddenly woke up from a very sound sleep. I immediately sat up in bed and said aloud, "Larry is dead." This was unusual behavior for me. I might toss and turn or lift myself on my elbow, but never sit up in bed like that. I thought to myself, *What a stupid idea. I know Larry is okay.* Then I lay back down and went to sleep.

The following afternoon, two Marines visited Larry's parent's home and delivered a death message. Larry had been killed in action by a mortar.

*   * *   *

I was working as a trooper at the Flint Post. One day as I drove to work, I thought how amazing it was that with such a large population living in the city, none of the police officers had ever hit any pedestrians. At the speeds we sometimes traveled during the course of our duties, it seemed remarkable. Within two hours after the start of my shift, I was involved in a pedestrian accident. Fortunately the person was not seriously hurt.

*   * *   *

Many years ago, I was investigating the death of a twenty-two-year-old male. The victim lived with his parents, though he was home alone when the accident occurred. His mother returned home to find her son dead in the dining room, with a .22 caliber rifle near his body.

While conducting my investigation, I eliminated homicide as the cause of death. However, I didn't think it was a suicide either. Not having much confidence in our Detective Bureau at the time, I did not request a detective right away. I felt the detective would write it off as a suicide. Yet, I could not figure out how his death had happened.

This case bothered me. It kept me awake. I lay in bed thinking about it. I could not let this nice family believe their son had deliberately killed himself if he had not. Finally, one night, I fell into a restless sleep. In my dreams, I reviewed my interview notes and revisited the scene. I analyzed and assessed the information I had over and over again in my mind—even though I was in a dream-like state. Suddenly I awakened. I knew what had happened.

When I went to work the next day, my shift sergeant suggested I talk to a detective, just to protect myself from legal responsibility. I chose the detective I had the most confidence in and told him what I believed happened. After I told him my theory, I went to the autopsy while he went back to the scene to check it out.

I believed that the victim, while his mother was gone, started cleaning his .22 caliber rifle. One of his brothers told me the weapon occasionally jammed, and a round could be left in the gun. The dining room had a wooden circular chandelier. I believe the victim held the weapon up to the light from the chandelier to check the barrel for cleanliness. He probably held the feeder latch open with his thumb. Then, he accidentally struck the chandelier with the butt of the rifle, his finger slipped off the latch, and the latch fell shut. With a jammed round left in the weapon, the weapon went off and struck the victim in the heart.

The detective confirmed this theory by locating an indentation in the wooden chandelier. It matched the edge of the butt of the gun. There was also some varnish on the butt of the gun from the wood of the chandelier. As confirmed in the autopsy, the angle of the wound through the heart was the exact angle that proved my theory. I solved the mystery while I was asleep.

The Children

I was temporarily living in a rental home I owned on Detroit's Eastside. I was in my mid-twenties, a police officer and also a Naval Reservist. One evening I fell asleep and had a dream:

I heard noises coming from the basement. I walked down the basement stairs and, as I entered the laundry room, observed a boy and a girl, both about eight years old. They were each dressed in beautiful clothing, as if going to church. However, they were transparent. I knew they had passed on. They, however, did not know they were ghosts.

As I entered the room, they looked at me and smiled. One child asked me, "Do you know where my daddy went? He was a Marine." At that moment, I observed a bright light at the top of the stairs, unlike any light I had ever seen before. It was brilliant.

I told the children, "I know where your daddy went. He went into the light. You have to go there, too." I held out my hands and the children reached for me, but their hands passed through mine. They smiled and we began walking up the stairs toward the light. As I approached, I couldn't enter any farther into the light; but I watched as the children passed by me and entered into the beautiful light.

Then I woke up. I couldn't believe how real the dream seemed. I told my roommate about it.

A few days later we were working in the basement, installing a 220-volt power outlet for a new high-powered air conditioner. The cable for the outlet had to be fed into the wall and ran from the upstairs living room to the basement—to the laundry room where I saw the children in my dream.

I cut a hole in the wall in the laundry room. As I reached into the wall to feed in the new cable, I felt something embedded in the wall. I pulled out a bayonet from a WWII rifle, still in its leather sheath! It was stamped U.S. 1941.

The bayonet had been sealed into the wall, right where I dreamed seeing the children. I considered it a gift from the children and their father for helping them get home. I still have it today.

Note: Although this officer was off duty when the events occurred, his story is included because it is an amazing one.

A Clairvoyant Dream

On September 11, 2001, I woke up and went for a walk with my sister in the early morning hours. We both wanted to get in better shape, so we power walked around the Civic Center track. I was tired and straggled behind her. "I'm so sorry," I said, "but I had this awful dream last night. When I woke up, I was just *exhausted!*" Since we always told our dreams to each other, I proceeded to tell her about mine.

"I was in the middle of a revolution. I was in a war. I think a bomb was dropped on us. I was with all these people I didn't know. We were running, and then we stopped. We just huddled together in this building. It was so dark. Parts of the building were falling all around us. There was smoke and fire everywhere, and I couldn't breathe. I was gasping for air. We ran down the stairs but were suddenly stopped. We were trapped, with no way out. It was horrible. I knew I was going to die—and I gave up! I've never had a dream like this before."

My sister listened attentively, and as we finished up our walk we tried to interpret the dream. Neither of us could imagine what it meant. We both thought maybe I had remembered an event from another lifetime.

When I arrived at work at eight, I wrote an e-mail to a friend downstate. I told him about my dream. I just couldn't let go of it. It was so unsettling.

I had no sooner sent the e-mail when my partner came into my office. He was agitated and said, "An airplane has just crashed into one of the Twin Towers!" I thought little of it. It was probably a student pilot that went off course and somehow hit the building.

About twenty minutes later, my partner ran into my office again, this time distraught. He gasped, "Another plane just crashed into the other building! They are *airliners!* I think we're being attacked!"

My heart fell to the floor and my stomach turned over as I remembered my dream from last night. I hurried to the conference room where everyone was watching the TV, and saw the smoke and the fire spewing out of the buildings.

The room was silent. No one uttered a word. I started shaking my head, nearly crying, and blurted, "The buildings are both going to fall down. There are thousands of people still inside them!" We were all sick to our stomachs. We stood there, watching as the buildings came down. It was awful.

I believe there is a connection between all policemen. We have the same mission—to help others. We are a family. We feel the excitement and the pain of our brothers. I think, somehow, I tuned into my police family when I had that dream. I felt their distress and I lived some of the chaos with them before it happened. What disturbed me most was meeting death and accepting its inevitability.

That day, hundreds of policemen and rescue workers died. Ultimately it affected the country and the whole world. The profound importance to our national and global life must have been a factor that triggered my vision.

I wonder how a person can move out of the confines of time and live a few moments in the future. I don't have the answers— but I know I was there.

Dream Warning

Police work seems to attract young men who have big egos and want to be macho. In Recruit School the cadets think they know everything. They show off their genitalia, belch, burp, and fart in the classroom (only when the instructor leaves the room, of course). I was certainly one of these guys. I thought I was so smart. And, since I'd shot rifles and shotguns ever since I was a kid, I thought I knew all about handguns, too.

After one particularly stressful ten-hour day of lectures and classes on defensive tactics and lifesaving techniques, running, and shooting on the range—I was tired. It seems when I'm tired, I dream a lot.

The dream I had that night concerned my pistol, which I had received just two days before.

I have returned to my elementary school and am in the classroom of one of my favorite teachers. I tell the teacher, "I'm here, policing at the school now. I'm here to guard the kids."

As I'm walking the hallways, a gangbanger sneaks into the school and I hear a commotion coming from my former teacher's classroom. I run into the room and pull out my handgun as I see the robber trying to take off with the teacher's money. Unfortunately, my gun falls apart, right in my hand! I am embarrassed. I can't believe this is happening in front of my role-model teacher. The gangster escapes through a window while mooning the class.

I wake up thinking, Damn! Some cop I am!

The next day I am tired but prepared for early morning hallway inspection. This is when all the recruits stand at attention next to the door of their bedrooms while police instructors stop in front of each recruit to inspect them. We know "inspection" is a game.

Most of us never take anything personally. Instructors like to yell at you, just to see if you can take it. We simply deal with it.

So, I'm standing by my door with my pistol in my right hand, both arms hanging by my sides. The rule is, as soon the instructor turns to face you, your right hand comes straight up from the elbow, so that your weapon is pointing straight up. The goal is to be sharp and quick about it.

Our new guns are Sig Saur 9MM handguns. I had cleaned mine the night before. Cleaning requires taking it completely apart, dousing it with gun cleaner, brushing it, wiping it, pulling a rod and pad through it, applying oil, and then putting it back together again. No big deal. I had cleaned long guns all my life.

As soon as the instructor faces me, my elbow goes up (quickly and sharply, I might add). In one split-second jerk, the slide flies off like an elongated bullet and hits the instructor square in the NUTS! *Oops.* I cringe. My fellow peers are snickering.

The whole friggin' gun falls apart! Every itty-bitty piece tumbles to the floor.

The instructor grabs his groin and I realize my dream has come true. I have embarrassed myself in front of one of my favorite instructors. I wasn't feeling macho anymore. I had forgotten to lock one simple part.

My dream had warned me, but I didn't listen. And, I soon realized my nightmare had just begun—I did push-ups for the remainder of Recruit School.

A Mother's Dream

In March 2004, the Manistique Public Safety Department went through a huge upheaval due to financial difficulties experienced by the city of Manistique. One officer got laid off, the director was forced to retire, and our fulltime dispatcher/clerk was cut back to four hours a day. This meant that our fulltime department of ten personnel lost twenty-five percent of its workforce. Although my position was still that of sergeant, my title was now the Acting Director of Manistique Public Safety.

One of our desires, as a department, was to change our uniforms. The current uniforms were outdated: light-blue shirts with French-blue pants. We never wore ties, except for court appearances—the uniform looked sloppy. After polling the officers, we unanimously voted to change to a dark-blue uniform —LAPD style. The officers even agreed to purchase the uniforms with their own money.

The new uniforms arrived in time for the annual July Fourth parade and festivities in Manistique. As the commanding officer of our department, it was my duty to lead the parade.

After dressing in the new uniform that morning, I looked in the mirror and was impressed with the way I looked. I then remembered a dream my mother had told me about as tears welled up in my eyes . . .

My mother died in 1995. Throughout my childhood, my sister, father, and I were continually astounded by my mother's dreams, as many of them often came true.

In 1976, I graduated from college with a bachelor's degree in criminal justice. After working for several small departments, I joined the Manistique Public Safety Department in 1978 because it was a chance to move back to my hometown. Although I accepted the position, I did not want to stay in Manistique forever and was continually applying to larger departments, including the Michigan State Police. In fact, there were many times I longed to quit my position in Manistique. I always hoped that a dream job would open up—and I was given many other opportunities—the trouble was I could not make up my mind as to where to go.

In 1985, I was accepted by the Michigan State Police and started to make preparations to quit Manistique and enter the State Police Academy. I was not thoroughly convinced that this was a good move, however, and was torn about what to do (I also had another job offer pending with a sheriff's department). My job situation was causing me a lot of personal turmoil. To make matters more confusing, my boss advised me that if I stayed in Manistique, they were going to give me a detective's position within the department, and this was something I really wanted.

At the peak of my frustration, I stopped to see my mother for coffee. I had always been close to her and often used her as a sounding board and source of advice. Therefore, she was aware of my current dilemma. She told me that she had a dream about my job problem that she wanted to tell me about.

In her dream she saw me standing at attention with a group of officers. She said something was going on; there was a big "doing," like a parade or something. I immediately asked Mom where this was happening. She replied that it was in Manistique, though she did not know where. I then asked her what color uniform I was wearing. She replied, "Dark blue."

I was relieved because I thought it meant I would become a member of the Michigan State Police and be stationed in Manistique in the future. I said, "I'm with the State Police, right?"

"No, not the State Police," Mom said. "I know their uniforms and it is not theirs." My mother knew all of the uniforms well because my father ran a wrecker service, and Mom was his secretary. City police, state police, and sheriff officers visited their repair shop frequently. I pressed her for more details.

She stated again that the event was in town and we all looked very proud standing at attention. She also said I was the leader of the men and that our uniforms were dark blue, including the shirts, pants, and ties.

I just shook my head. I was absolutely certain Mom was wrong on this one—there was no way this dream could become true. Manistique Public Safety wore light-blue uniforms, and she had said I was not with the State Police. I told Mom she was wrong this time.

She looked at me, smiled, and shook her bony finger at me. "You'll see. This was a very strong dream. It will come true," she predicted.

As I stood in front of the mirror that morning, I realized the validity of Mom's dream so many years ago.

The Psychic Janitor

I was conducting a polygraph examination on a subject named Rudy Oliverze. Rudy was a white male who was related to a homicide suspect named Melvin Garza. Melvin was suspected in the disappearance of his girlfriend, Robin Adams, who was believed to have been murdered. The detective suspected that when the woman was babysitting for a friend, Garza came to the house, took the woman, killed her, and buried her. A few days elapsed before she was reported missing, so the investigation was cold from the beginning.

Rudy was being questioned to see if he had information, involvement, or knowledge concerning Robin's disappearance. We believed he might have helped Garza get rid of the body.

During my pre-test interview Rudy told me that his real name was Raul Oliverze. In making conversation, Raul described his wife, Kathy. She had long blonde hair, parted in the middle, and pulled back behind her head.

Raul failed the polygraph but made no admissions following the testing. However, once he left the examination room, I found out some interesting things. A detective from the Caro Post, who was sitting behind the window watching the polygraph, had been in touch with several psychics during the investigation. One psychic, who was a janitor at the Gaylord State Police post, approached him one day while he was gassing up his vehicle at the post. The psychic told the detective he had a dream and knew the detective was looking for a missing woman. (This conversation occurred well before I ran the polygraph.) Although the detective thought this was strange, he listened to the janitor because he was, indeed, conducting a homicide investigation.

The janitor stated that the woman was dead and buried. The psychic described a place in the woods, down a dirt road. He said the detective would find the spot if he followed the road and crossed a bridge. He would then need to turn right and go up a hill. He was to follow a fence with unusual white signs, and there, in a clearing, is where the woman was buried. He said the woman was buried in the fetal position and she was lying on her right side.

This psychic janitor also described someone who could have knowledge or may have helped bury the body. His name was Raul Alavez. Raul was married to a woman with long blonde hair that she pulled back on both sides. His wife's name would be Karen. This man, Raul, would have knowledge that would help solve the case.

The detective then told me that he did not know *Rudy's* real name was *Raul* until he heard it mentioned during the pre-test interview I just conducted. He said he recognized where the psychic said Robin was buried as he had visited the old grounds of the Caro Regional Center that morning. The white signs, fence, road, bridge and clearing he saw that morning matched what the janitor described.

Later, Robin's body was found near this location—just as the psychic janitor said it would be.

Trusting Your Instincts

As a young trooper, I started my career with the Michigan State Police at the Ypsilanti Post. After two years there, I asked for a transfer to the Upper Peninsula since my elderly parents and in-laws lived on the west end. I was assigned to the Stephenson Post in the Upper Peninsula.

One night my partner and I went to look for an individual for whom we had a warrant for furnishing intoxicants to minors. The wanted subject was known to be at his deer hunting camp as he knew we were looking for him. We went to the camp, only to find it dark, no vehicle around—apparently he was not there. We looked into the windows with flashlights. I could see fresh food on plates in the sink. After looking through several windows, only one more remained which had not been checked. At that point, I had a strong premonition that told me not to look in that window. My partner did not want to look in anymore windows, either. We left without incident.

The following day one of our officers arrested the subject. He told the trooper, "If that trooper last night had looked into the last window, I would have blown him away." He had been sitting in the dark with a loaded .30-06 waiting to shoot me.

After learning of his intentions, I knew why I had had such a strong feeling to not look in that last window. Apparently, my partner was also uncomfortable at the time, since he instructed me loudly not to investigate any further.

Reuben R. Johnson, Retired Lieutenant
Michigan State Police

The Trooper and the Banker

by Tom Brosman

Charley was a trooper
And he worked his beat with care.
His brother Danny was a banker
And a self-made millionaire.

Danny's office was in Bellevue
With a mahogany desk and a leather chair,
A twelve thousand dollar couch stood beside the wet bar there
And from twenty stories up he had a million dollar view.

Charley's office was a troop car
And beside his seat a .12 gauge stood.
He knew his beat from near to far
And he surveyed it across his Crown Vic's hood.

Danny went on trips to Spain
And Portugal and such.
Charley counted every dime
And after bills there wasn't much.

With Danny's pay, even after bills,
He put the bulk in stocks and bonds
And the banker thought about his brother
Who risked his life from dusk til dawn.

"Why on earth does Charley do it,
For so little in return?
He wears that badge so proudly
And for himself shows no concern.

I can drive down through Seattle
In my Jag or big Mercedes fast
And see the buildings that I've bankrolled pass
While my brother always faces battle.

What does Charley see in a life
That's chained to twenty-four by seven,

When he could live a life like mine
That is a double slice of heaven?"

Every 10th and 25th, Charley banked his trooper check
And thought of Danny who was buried in riches to his neck.
The trooper pondered about his life and living
And decided there wasn't a lot he was missing.

Yes, Danny dined on shrimp and steak
And Charley was happy for his brother.
But never in the trooper's dreams,
Would he trade places with the other.

For every building Danny built,
Charley savored his job's own thrills.
For all the DUIs he'd popped
Before someone was surely killed.

For twenty years Charley had worked
Between the doors and on the road.
He'd rolled to fatals, and crashes bad.
He had comforted the injured, the dying, the sad.

On the roads of his detachment's sector
His brother and sister troopers kept the peace.
They were law and strong protection
In rain and snow and wind and sleet.

"Why would Danny live a life soft and safe from strife?
With little purpose as far as I can see?
While I am dealing with death and life,
He is choosing between cheddar or brie."

I've lost all count of those I've helped
Or the number of lives I've saved.
All the speeders, the nights, the days,
And people stranded on dark highways.

So, my banker brother can think his thoughts
That his house and cars are super.
He can't comprehend the satisfaction brought,
By being a Washington State Trooper.

"Humor has justly been regarded as the finest perfection of poetic genius."

Thomas Carlyle

Healing With Humor

Humor is transpersonal. Comics who make thousands of people laugh at once go beyond one person. Since survival is the key in police work, laughing at ourselves and at human frailties helps lighten our load significantly. Humor is divine.

"What soap is to the body, laughter is to the soul."

Yiddish Proverb

"The human race has only one really effective weapon and that is laughter."

Mark Twain

"You can turn painful situations around through laughter. If you can find humor in anything—even poverty— you can survive it."

Bill Cosby

A Reportable Incident

My partner and I were sent on an unknown trouble call to an address in Saginaw. When we arrived we found a severely damaged garage and a man lying in his backyard, moaning and groaning on the ground next to a washer and dryer. Apparently the man had gotten out of the car to open the garage door so that his wife could drive the car into the garage. Her foot must have slipped off the brake and onto the accelerator. She drove her poor husband up onto the hood of the car, through the garage door, and all the way through the garage until it reached the back wall where the washer and dryer were located.

As we surveyed the damage to her husband and the garage his wife said, "I don't understand it. The harder I pressed on the brake, the faster the car went."

Then, she asked, "You don't suppose we will have to make a report on this, do you?"

Fresh Meat

One quiet summer night, about 2:00 A.M., my partner and I are driving in the middle of nowhere. There isn't a soul in sight. To say the least, there is no activity.

As I drive near a state game area I was familiar with, I decided to park the patrol car by an old covered-bridge that crossed over a small stream. The bridge was actually closed for safety reasons, but we could get out and stretch our legs.

I pulled the car to the side of the dirt road about halfway into the brush, and my partner and I got out to enjoy the fresh air and to take a break from driving in unproductive circles. We had been talking for a few minutes when a car came down the roadway toward the bridge. Two couples got out; we could hear their conversation clearly.

One couple decided to walk down the road a bit while the other couple stayed on the bridge. They would each have some time alone with their dates. The two couples agreed to meet back at the car in about forty-five minutes.

My partner and I were standing about twenty-five feet from the couple on the bridge. But it was incredibly dark and they had no idea there were two male troopers nearby.

We listened as the male tried to convince the female to have sex on the bridge. He pleaded and used every line in the book—it was all we could do to stifle our laughter. She kept saying things like "I don't like it out here. Trolls live under bridges and people get murdered. Just like in the horror movies."

He continued to reassure her that the area was safe and he was actually making a little progress toward his goal. He said, "There's nobody out here for miles. HELLOOO!" His voice echoed in the night.

My partner, who had a deep voice, howled back in his scariest voice, "Fressshhhh meeaatt!!!!!" The couple screamed in terror and ran for the car! They drove away fast, honking the horn for the other couple. We heard car doors slam down the road—but we were laughing too hard to know what was said.

It's a Bomb!

Report of a bomb threat in a large, crowded city park brings the Michigan State Police bomb squad running. The alleged bomb is hidden inside a McDonald's bag that has been carefully and strategically placed on a park bench.

Within minutes of the phone call, the entire bomb squad is in action. Big burly troopers wearing specialized suits and face-shields drive the armored truck into the park as close as they dare to the aforementioned park bench. In synchronized movements they guard the perimeter and advise the growing crowd of onlookers to be careful. "Stand behind the yellow tape! This is a dangerous situation—come no closer!" Typical cop talk. Typical cop activity: guarding citizens at all costs.

The audience is transfixed as the bomb squad brings out the new robot (which the state police are *very* proud of, by the way). It is carefully brought into position by remote control—actually, awesome technology to observe.

The robot's arm is slowly and strategically extended towards the paper bag. It is just about ready to pick up the bomb to place it in the truck for detonation when, out of nowhere, a seagull dives towards the bag, snatches it up, and flies away with it!

The bomb squad starts shouting and cussing at the scavenger. Some members grab their radios, trying to communicate with headquarters on how to best handle this change of events. Other officers scratch their heads in disbelief ... and yet others start to chase the bird.

"Hey—follow that bird!"

"No, *shoot* it!"

"NOOO! We can't shoot it, the bomb will blow up!"

"If it lands in the tree, then shoot it."

"He's still flying, *dumb-ass!*"

"Uh, oh . . . oh no . . . he's landing . . ."

"Oh, NO! He's pecking at the bag!"

"RUN, Forrest, RUN!!!!"

Each time the bird lands, the crowd scatters in all directions. No sooner does everyone get re-situated then the gull changes its mind and flies off again! The bird does this at least three times, as if only looking for a wee bit of privacy to enjoy its prize.

Since the bag has not yet exploded, Trooper Forrest finally says, "Hmm, maybe it's not a bomb . . ."

The bird eventually lands long enough to start pecking at the bag. As the bomb squad and crowd watch in anticipation, the seagull tears open the bag with its bill and pulls out a half-eaten hamburger and some French fries! The empty McDonald's bag begins to drift away on the breeze, as onlookers laugh and clap and cackle. "Maybe you better chase the empty bag now, troopers!" Then someone offers, "I know—shoot the bird for *littering!*"

Embarrassed, tired, and silent, the state troopers begin to load up the million-dollar robot. One of the officers picks up the bag and throws it in a nearby trash can.

If they hadn't experienced it themselves, this specially trained group of men would not imagine it possible for one small bird to bring an entire bomb squad to its knees.

The Fatality

It was not uncommon for me to be twenty or thirty miles away from a call or an accident. One day the dispatcher reported a rollover accident—possible fatal—and requested a car respond. I radioed in and drove to the scene even though I was more than half an hour away.

When I arrived, I saw a car had rolled over onto its roof. There was no one inside. I did, however, find one body that had apparently been thrown from the car lying nearby, face up in the ditch. The strange thing is that the man's legs and arms were crossed. This was unusual. I couldn't help but notice how peaceful he looked. He was deader than a doornail, but he looked peaceful.

Fatal accidents require hours of tedious and time-consuming investigating. Pictures must be taken, sketches made, and measurements noted. The investigator may have to re-create the accident scene in a courtroom several years after the fact, so I requested assistance from an accident reconstructionist from the crime laboratory. This will be a five-hour report before it is over, I thought.

After I roped off the area and set out some flares, I returned to the car. As I was sitting in the cruiser, writing notes and recording data, an old Cadillac hearse pulled up. Two men were inside. They parked in front of me, waved hello, and smiled as they got out. I watched as they walked over to the body. Each man grabbed a limb and they started to carry the dead man toward the hearse.

To say the least, I was surprised. I jumped out of my car and raced over them. "What the hell do you think you are doing?" I bellowed. "Put that body back just the way you found it and get the hell out of here!" I made it clear that I had not summoned a hearse and wouldn't need them at least for a few more hours. I would call them when their services were needed.

The driver and the assistant stood there, dumbfounded. At six feet four inches and 225 pounds, they were not about to challenge me. They could see I was not in a good mood and meant business. They returned to the hearse. After several minutes, one of them eased out of the vehicle and approached me. He said, "We were en route from our funeral home near Ft. Wayne, Indiana. We were transporting the body of a man who passed away the day before yesterday. We happened to come across this rollover just after it happened. Both the driver and one occupant were injured. Our hearse was full and there is more money in transporting injured people than dead people, so we put the dead guy in the ditch, loaded up the two injured individuals, and raced them to the hospital. Now, we are returning to pick up the original body."

I have had serious-injury accidents that turned into fatals; however, I never had a fatal accident that turned into an injury accident! Just goes to show, anything can happen!

Note: In the 1960s, just about every small-town funeral home used its hearse as an ambulance when they were not using it as a hearse. This helped pay bills and gave morticians something to do in their spare time. I don't imagine you would see something like this happen today.

Critters I Have Caught

When I worked for a rural sheriff's office fifty miles south of the Mackinaw Bridge, we had to do it all . . . if a citizen called, we went. No request went unanswered. I have chased many a critter in my day!

One quiet afternoon the dispatcher called me on the radio to say, "Mr. Smith has a strange looking pig in his garden and he wants it out—NOW!" I remember the look on the pig's face when it saw me. It smiled as if to say, "Catch me if you can, Copper!" I could tell it was none too happy to have its afternoon snack interrupted by an angry gardener—let alone me! Imagine a deputy sheriff in full uniform chasing a pot-bellied pig around the yard. After a not-so-high-speed chase, I gave up wearing those shiny patent leather shoes and stuck with boots (it got a little messy). But, with the grace of God and the help of two neighbor kids, we got that pig in custody!

*   * *   *

One morning a lady called to complain that her neighbor's chickens were in her yard again, harassing her dog and eating the dog's food. Well, duty calls . . . so with some Joe Montana moves I learned from watching football on TV, there I was, with a big ol' fishing net in my hand, chasing squawking chickens as they ran all over the yard, flapping their wings with feathers flying.

A County Mountie never gives up until the job is done! I took all thirteen birds into custody and transported them to the local animal shelter. The owner of the chickens had to bail them out the next day. After a day locked up in the pen, the chickens were rehabilitated, and the neighbor lady and her dog never had trouble with those pesky fowl again!

* ** *

I was patrolling in Onaway, a small village twenty-some miles away from where a motorist had reported almost hitting a small bear that was wandering around a busy highway like it was drunk. By the time I arrived, the scene was packed with onlookers, deputies, city police officers, a state trooper, firemen, and ambulance personnel. It looked like a big emergency with everybody but the SWAT team present!

As I walked closer, I saw the bear sitting on its butt, swaying like a drunken sailor. Every time the bear tried to stand up, all of the onlookers and emergency service personnel would run back to the safety of their vehicles. The bear did not look that big to me. I decided it must be sick and needed to see a vet.

Well, the local vet was out of town, so that meant Mr. Bear had to go for a nice ride. I requested another officer bring up the ACO truck and all the catch-all poles he could find. Luckily it was Sunday because Mary, a friend of mine who runs the animal shelter in a neighboring town, was nearby visiting her mother. I got on the radio and advised dispatch to call Mary at her mother's and tell Mary I needed help with a bear.

When Mary arrived, the two of us approached the bear with catch-all poles in our hands and got him moving. None of the "brave men" would come near as we walked him to the back of the ACO truck. Finally, we got a little help to hoist the bear into the truck. It was a sobering moment.

Mr. Bear immediately started rocking the entire truck, trying to get out of the enclosed box. Mary and I transported it to the animal shelter in the next county (the truck rocked the whole way!) and requested a few deputies be there to assist us when we unloaded it.

When we arrived at the shelter, two deputies were waiting—they really did not want to be there. When we opened the truck and got the catch-all poles back on the bear, so we could drag him into the building, the two male deputies drew their service weapons and kept them trained on the bear—just in case. They did not want to get too close to it or touch it. So, just the two of us, Mary and me, dragged the bear from the truck into the shelter. We got the bear in and locked him down.

The next day when Mary went to check on the bear, she opened the door and he was gone. Her heart almost stopped. She looked up, and there he was—he had climbed up to the top of the fence in the holding cell. Eventually, the vet checked over the bear and found it had gotten into ant poison that someone had used outside his house. After the bear went through de-tox, it was fine. Before the bear was returned to the wild, a tracking collar was put on him.

For several years afterward, every time I ran into a DNR friend of mine, he would give me an update on how the bear was doing. At the time of the incident the bear weighed ninety-nine pounds . . . he is much larger now.

The Doper

A long-haired doper visited his eighteen-year-old girlfriend while she was working at a pizza parlor. She was busy cutting up veggies when he walked in. She had recently heard that he was two-timing her so she confronted him. He admitted he was. She was upset that they had been having unprotected sex and that she could have contracted HIV.

The knucklehead said, "Well, we all have to go some time." When he turned to walk away, she buried a paring knife right in his back!

Unaware of what she had done, he got into his car and drove away. When he finally leaned back in the seat to get out, he realized that a knife was in his back. An ambulance was called and my partner and I were dispatched to investigate.

This creepy victim was known to have loud parties all night, every night. When his neighbors, who were out milling around, heard that he had been stabbed and would be in the hospital overnight, they were happy because they would finally get an uninterrupted night's sleep.

We were standing at the back of the ambulance when another neighbor came home from work and walked over to see what the commotion was. When he heard that Mr. Knucklehead had been stabbed with a paring knife and had driven all the way home with it stuck in his back, he asked us, "Can't you arrest him for driving while im-pared?"

Trooper Daniel Caviston, Retired
Michigan State Police

In loving memory of Captain Gary McGhee, Michigan State
Police, retired, who recently passed away.

When Bad Blood is Good

It is May 1966. The Harrison Road Headquarters is the first Police Recruit School in the state to serve cafeteria meals to its entire compound. This is not necessarily a positive thing for the recruits.

We affectionately call the head cook "Ptomaine Tom." The food is tasteless and on Thursday nights we are served nasty cold cuts for supper. Little did I guess the unappealing fare would actually benefit me one day.

One afternoon, when we were well into the term at the school, I reported for a demerit lap and was standing rigidly at attention between the carpenter shop and the gym. I thought I might have missed something, as there was no one else around. After I had stood there for what seemed like an eternity, Trooper Michael Anderson (later Major Mike) opened the window of the beloved "head" and barked, "McGHEE, WHAT ARE YOU DOING OUT THERE? RECRUIT McGHEE!" He had plenty of reason to know my name by now.

"SIR . . . RECRUIT McGHEE, SIR. WAITING TO RUN MY DEMERIT, SIR," was my reply.

"AREN'T YOU GOING TO THE RED CROSS TO GIVE BLOOD?" was his next inquiry—in a voice that indicated I was.

So, that is what I had missed. The entire recruit school had been scheduled to go to the Red Cross to donate blood. In my most courageous voice, I replied, "SIR, RECRUIT McGHEE, SIR. NO, SIR."

Anderson's response was immediate and condemning. "WHY NOT, McGHEE?" I could tell we were about to become even better acquainted.

85

"SIR, RECRUIT McGHEE, SIR. I NEED ALL I HAVE, SIR."
"GET UP HERE, MCGHEE," was his prompt reply.
"SIR. YES, SIR!"

The entire school, including yours truly, was loaded onto the bus, and off to the Red Cross we were taken. No attention was paid to our screaming and kicking.

After our arrival, we took turns having our finger stabbed (not pricked) by a nurse who had obviously been recently divorced from a state trooper. After poking a hole in my finger and squeezing a pint of blood into a tube of unidentifiable liquid, something was supposed to happen.

Now, mind you, I don't know *what* was supposed to happen, but in my case, it did *not* happen. This was good news to me, as I didn't want to be separated from any more of my blood.

Come to find out, all but *three* of the brave souls in Recruit School had the same result! The Red Cross staff advised the department that the recruits had insufficient iron in their blood for donation purposes.

My blood supply owed a debt of gratitude to "Ptomaine Tom." The ultimate outcome was predictable. Recruits began to receive a better quality of food . . . including meats and other sources of iron. We were appreciative, of course, but we never did go back to donate blood.

Mama!

Editor's Note: The humor in this story is not the demise of the victim, but rather Elmer's sudden reaction to an almost inconceivable moment. It was the visual of poor Elmer running out. Cops have a strange sense of humor that sometimes only other cops understand, but it is to cope with, minimize, and heal from certain unexpected moments like this.

Late one night, my partner and I received a call on a possible suicide. The subject had been despondent and neighbors reported hearing a single gunshot from within the house.

As we drove up, we saw Elmer walking inside the house. Elmer was a large man and had been with the local city police department since the 1950s when he started out as a volunteer. Eventually he was grandfathered into the department and never received much formal training. Elmer was a nice guy.

As my partner and I were walking up the front walkway, we heard Elmer suddenly shriek, "MAMA!" and like a shot, he crashed through the front screen door and took it off its hinges. We immediately took cover, thinking the person inside was going to shoot at us. Poor Elmer was shaking and trembling all over. At first, he couldn't speak.

When he finally got control of himself, he told us what happened. He had entered the house and found the man face down in a large pool of blood with a shotgun beside him. The lights were out. After some time, Elmer finally shined his flashlight on the dead body, when the man unexpectedly lifted his head and said, "Heeelp meee . . ." It was a horror-flick moment as the man was missing half of his face! The shotgun had only done half the job.

The man survived and so did Elmer. We only laugh at the vision of chubby Elmer frantically crashing through the door.

Hopeful Journey

by Tom Brosman

Five were from Seattle
The sixth cadet from Orcas Isle
Seven were from farms with wheat and cattle
One drove a Lexus to Shelton in style.

Spokane sent four sons and daughters
Pullman two and one from Kettle Falls
One came from Longview, beside Columbia's waters
A lineman from Richland sent his only daughter

There were forty-three cadets in all
From cities and farms and boonies
They all traveled to Shelton
To form a class of newbies

Some had good cars and money to spend
Some bummed rides from a friend
They left behind all they knew
Some were scared and lonely, too

Most were nervous about the future at the WSP
Oh, they had heard of washouts at the Academy
Each wanted to be the best—and more
But they felt alone as they entered the academy's door

Yes, they were alone and keenly felt it
As they eyed the other cadets with just as far to go
But life is seldom what you think at the time
And how could they know, the green cadets standing in the line?

They drilled and saluted, and drilled and drilled again
And sweated beside each other, the women and the men
They went to EVOC class and learned to PIT a car
Domestic violence, changing flats, and more

Three cadets were cut, then two more
From a class that was learning and growing full bore
Those who remained in that class
Found they needed each other to pass

No longer strangers from far away
They were comrades who helped each other stay
Months later, they got their commissions
And hoped their dream lists were not illusions

They became troopers for the state of Washington
And took their places with others more seasoned
They worked their beats and honed their skills
Most looked back to Academy days fondly still

To their first days as cadets so green
With strangers as different as they could be
Whom time and pressure made so dear
Friendships strong, abiding, sincere.

Life did have a joke to play
About how they felt on that very first day
About those "strangers" who were in their way
Who would cheer for them, protect them til retirement day

The cadets from that class in Shelton
When life was looking kind of barren
Would share their comrades' highs and lows on life's trapeze
When things were going well, or they were in the grease

That Academy class, troopers now, work between the doors
From Idaho's green border to Westport's wave-tossed shore
Writing citations, working fatals, doing reports, and more
Most are grateful for their hopeful journey that began at the Academy
    door

Lessons of the Heart

Emotional intelligence as a quality of the infinite Self goes far beyond our ego; it goes beyond Freud's superego of conditioning and habituation. It is not just a counterbalance or an opposite of our IQ. It is powerful. The integration of both the rational and the intuitive comprises the full extent of our aptitude. Some people have a high degree of intelligence in both areas, while others have little of either. I believe police officers in particular have the potential of becoming highly developed because they are forced to use both their rational and emotional intelligence to stay alive. Police officers see things that most people never experience.

"We now have scientific evidence that the heart sends us emotional and intuitive signals to help govern our lives. . . . Because of this new evidence, we have to rethink our entire attitude toward 'following our hearts.' . . . As a society, we need to take the concept of heart out of confinement in religion and philosophy and put it right in the 'street', where it's needed most. The heart isn't mushy or sentimental. It's intelligent and powerful, and we believe that it holds the promise for the next level of human development and for the survival of our world."

Doc Childre and Howard Martin with Donna Beech,
Beyond the Brain: The Intelligent Heart

What Child Is This?

It was the middle of the night. The bars had just closed. I arrived at the scene of a single-car accident. A car had a hit a telephone pole with such impact that the telephone pole was completely obliterated and was lying horizontal on the ground. The car was resting on its roof. The lights from my patrol car intermittently shined on the vehicle, and I could hear emergency vehicle sirens on their way.

The female driver was thrown from the vehicle. It was apparent that she had been drinking. I could smell intoxicants on her breath as she lay motionless—actually sleeping—on the ground nearby. I attempted to talk with her, but she was so drunk she didn't even know she had been in an accident.

As the ambulance neared, I looked at the mangled vehicle, thinking how lucky the woman was to be alive. I don't know what it was, but something drew my eyes to the vehicle's interior, just as the patrol car lights lit up the scene like a strobe. I saw a little boy—standing erect, his feet firmly planted on the interior of the upside-down roof! Amazed, I blinked my eyes to focus. He was only about three feet tall, probably about four years old. Each time the light shined on the car, I saw him.

I ran to the car and searched for a large enough opening so I could reach him with my arms. He didn't seem to know I was there. He was in shock. He just stood straight up, like a soldier at attention. He was sniffling and quietly moaning, as if he had been taught not to cry. His left arm looked broken and limp as he held it.

I reached through a crumpled window and carefully lifted the boy. Wonderingly, I took him out of the vehicle and cradled him in my arms, as though he were my own son. I gave him a teddy bear that I carry in the patrol car and said, "There now, everything will be all right." He clutched the stuffed animal with his right arm, as though he would never let it go.

After inspecting the scene, I couldn't figure out where the boy had come from. How did he survive the accident? The car was hardly recognizable. How could I have missed him inside that mangled mess? There was no blood on him. Was he thrown from the vehicle and then walked back in? Or did he end up in a seat and then extricate himself?

There is nothing terribly more significant about this incident, except that I will never forget the vision of him standing inside that car, alone, hurt, and confused.

Love Train

Skagway, Alaska, a town with little more than 850 residents, is nestled within an impressive array of mountains that claw at the sky. These rugged peaks provide a nearly impassible barrier to the Canadian interior.

Today, in early spring, when lawns have turned green and lower elevation trees explode with new life, the old steam engine is brought out of storage for the season's first run through White Pass over a narrow-gauge track that was installed in 1897. This is always a highly publicized event, with many local residents riding the inaugural trip over the pass. Old Number 73 has left the station and begins its long journey toward White Pass.

I am working the 4:00 P.M. to midnight shift, fighting a bout of cynicism and generally feeling sorry for myself. All the problems associated with a twenty-something life surge through my head. Even in the land of my dreams, Alaska, the thought of life passing me by is overpowering. As I drive up to the railroad shops on Skagway's north end, I am in no mood for the strange vehicle that is parked beyond the cluttered buildings.

The car sits alongside the tracks, far beyond the rail yards and near the Gold Rush Cemetery. From a distance, I can see two people in the front seat. The car is an old Chevy Nova which, apparently, has driven its share of bad roads. A battered Yukon license plate hangs awkwardly from the rear bumper.

Suddenly angry, I drive toward the car grudgingly, feeling obligated to investigate the suspicious intruder. As I slowly pull up from behind, Old Number 73 is picking up speed. In my present mood, I am already furious with the vehicle's occupants for forcing me to provide police service. I park at the rear bumper and angrily exit my unit.

A poorly dressed middle-aged man steps from the car and meets me halfway. He seems to be somewhat embarrassed. "Am I doing something wrong, officer?" he asks, avoiding eye contact while looking down the tracks.

"Let's see some identification," I scowl.

"Yes, ah, sure, officer. Anything you want." He pulls out a battered leather wallet from his pocket and removes a Yukon driver's license.

"Canyon?" I say, surprised he has traveled so far in this wreck of a car.

"Yes, sir. I was able to get my shift at the mine covered. We headed out this morning," he replied, still looking for the oncoming train.

"So . . . what brings you to Skagway?" I sarcastically ask, more out of annoyance than suspicion.

"My son likes to see the train. It's kind of special for him. He's been waiting all winter for the first run."

I look beyond the Nova and can see black smoke from Old Number 73 slowly making its way up the tracks. At least the train will pass soon and they'll leave, I think, wishing the locomotive would hurry. They weren't doing anything wrong, minor trespassing perhaps, but nothing serious. I just wanted them gone and out of my hair. Forcing myself to continue the investigation, I bend over and look inside the car at the guy's son, expecting to see a young boy.

He must have been about my age. A birth defect has caused his present condition. Weak neck muscles are unable to support his head, and it flops from side to side, but he is constantly looking down the tracks. Skinny arms with twisted hands uncontrollably swat at nothing. A long string of drool drains from his mouth to a large wet spot on his collarless shirt.

A battered wheelchair lays in the backseat, folded, to complete this depressing collage.

"Train, Daddy! Train, Daddy!" he spits out with glee.

The train is indeed approaching, as I stand quietly with absolutely nothing to say.

"We drive down each year for the first run of the season," the man says, looking distantly at the approaching smoke. "My son likes trains. He likes the rumble they make."

Mentally, I beg him to stop talking. I have heard enough.

"We left early this morning. The trip takes a long time because we have to stop a lot."

Please, just shut up. I don't want to hear anymore, I scream to myself.

"It sure does make him happy. Whenever he sees a train on TV or in a book, he smiles. This one's his favorite though."

Inside I struggle for something to say, but words won't come. Five minutes ago I was filled with anger—and now, three hundred seconds later, I am awash in emotions I hardly understand.

"Train, Daddy! Train!" his son squeals, his hands flailing up and down.

Old Number 73 roars by us like black thunder, shaking the rail bed with heavy antique power. The boy laughs and screeches as his father walks around to be near him at the passenger door. I watch father and son share a moment of simple joy. A joy I took for granted, at least until today.

He is not a man of money, of that I am certain. The day off work is no doubt one without pay and will surely affect his monthly bills. But, he loves his son so much he has sacrificed this day to please him. I feel sick inside. *How could I be so self-involved?* My mind swims with various biblical passages from my youth, each fitting this scene like a glove.

Self-sacrifice and undying love—a lesson is being learned, right here, right now. I can feel it inside me.

I watch the pair as the train finally passes and disappears around the curve. Choking back tears, I walk toward them. Still excited, his son is trying to call back the train. They face a six-hour drive after this brief moment of joy. I have a sudden urge to do something. I owe it to them for my self-righteousness, but am having trouble keeping my composure.

"Old Number 73 will be back in about an hour. You get to see it again before we go home," the man says, smiling down at his son, who claps and squeals as he squirms around in the seat.

I am pacing in a circle. I want to leave. This is not a comfortable situation for me. *That was it! I was not comfortable! My God,* I thought, *what have I become?*

"Sir, once the train is back at the station, it will make another run tonight. Would you and your son like to ride up the pass?" I ask, determined to make up for my internal cynicism.

The man frowns and walks away quickly from the car. He lowers his voice, so his son cannot hear.

"I checked on the tickets officer. They're very expensive. I only have enough gas money to get home," he says, looking at the dusty ground.

"Don't worry, sir," I reply as I wipe the corner of one eye. "The conductor owes me a favor. I'll get you both on for free."

"You sure officer? You don't have to do that." He is staring much too directly into my eyes.

"Yes, I do, sir," I say, hoping he will not ask me any more questions. "You wait here with your son and watch the train return, and then meet me at the train station. I'll take care of everything."

"My son will like that a lot," he says, looking away.

"I know he will." I turn to leave while I can still talk.

I drive to the railroad office and find a parking space among the many vehicles in the lot. I had lied about the conductor's favor—I purchase two passes for the next ride.

Tourists are pouring out of the parlor cars when the father and son arrive at the station. It is not easy to get his son loaded in the observation seat, but we manage.

Standing back on the outside step, I watch these two people become so excited for what others take for granted. I love the way I feel inside. My own concerns are fading away and becoming insignificant.

Minutes later, the engine belches black smoke and the whistle blows its evening song.

Before leaving the station, I purchase some train souvenirs and pick up a brochure displaying Old Number 73. The man had locked his car, but my slim-jim tool quickly takes care of that obstacle. After I place the items on the front seat and relock the car door, I return to patrolling—with an inner peace I hadn't felt in a long time.

Excerpt from the book *Alaska Behind Blue Eyes* by Alan L. White. For more information, visit www.alanlwhite.com

In loving memory of Sergeant Dennis Finch, Traverse City
Police Department, who died in the line of duty.

Denny

I am not a religious person, though I am cognizant of unexplained happenings and the uncanny timing of certain events. My deepest questioning about "the order of things" occurred when my friend Denny Finch was shot and killed by John Clark, a mentally deranged individual.

John Clark's neighbor phoned 911. Something was wrong. John was pacing in his yard with a gun. She considered him dangerous and was concerned about her and her neighbors' welfare. Denny answered the call and offered his assistance since he had talked with John many times before.

When Denny arrived at the Clark's home, John was delusional. He thought the police were the Mafia and that Denny was sent as the hit man.

Unknown to Denny or any of the local police, John had an arsenal of weapons and ammunition in his basement that included both automatic and semi-automatic long guns and pistols—even a .50-caliber sniper rifle.

I was finishing my shift and getting ready to unload when I heard Central Dispatch request a patrol unit to guard a neighborhood intersection. There were not many details given out over the radio, but I decided to answer the call. After sitting in the patrol car at the intersection for about forty-five minutes I figured out there was a man with a gun and that police were evacuating nearby houses.

As I wondered what had inspired me to guard this particular intersection, I noticed an elderly couple walking their little dog. They seemed to be heading towards the standoff. Even though they were two blocks away from me, I felt compelled to stop them. I quickly ran up to them and said, "Excuse me, Sir. Ma'am. Please . . ."

Before I could finish warning them, a barrage of gunshots rang out—so loudly and in such close proximity that I dove for the nearest tree!

Suddenly I realized I was only ten feet from the gunman, who was standing in the front doorway of his house. I looked in back of me—*the entire police perimeter was behind me!* In my attempt to protect the couple walking their dog, I had put myself in the middle of a gun battle!

At that point, Denny backed out of the doorway and fell down backwards on the porch. The deranged man was still standing in the doorway, with an assault rifle in his hands. I drew my weapon and fired several rounds at him. I knew Denny had been shot several times and I wanted to get to him. John disappeared through the doorway, so I thought I had hit him with one of the rounds from my gun.

The porch where Denny lay was about three feet off the ground. I quickly crawled to the edge, which had a thick railing around it. I was about twelve inches from Denny's face. He was moaning. I could see that he had been peppered with bullets from head to toe and that he was unable to help himself in any way. (I found out later he was shot twenty-three times.)

Denny begged me, "Get me off of this porch, *please.* I don't want to die like this. Get me off of this porch! *Please!*"

There is something about looking into a dying man's face and feeling his pain. I knew I had to do something. However, the only way to get Denny off the porch was to go up the steps, walk in front of the doorway, turn left, and then drag him back down the steps. The railing around the porch was so thick I couldn't possibly pull Denny through or over it.

I knew the suspect could shoot me—but the need to help Denny was greater than my fear.

So, I just did it! I was petrified. I counted, "One. Two. Three. Go!" I ran so fast up the stairs, I nearly broke my nose! I plowed into the side of the house before I turned left, then grabbed Denny under the armpits, and dragged him down the steps halfway across the front lawn.

I had wanted to move Denny in a "rescue carry" over my shoulder, but his one leg was almost severed. I was afraid it would fall off. His leg was only dangling on muscle and skin. Denny was not wearing a vest and he had been mercilessly shot up. I had to keep him close to the ground so his limbs would not fall off due to gravity.

At this point, John reappeared in the doorway. Apparently, I hadn't hit him—he had merely gone back downstairs to get another weapon as one of my bullets had jammed his gun.

Fortunately I had enough time to move Denny to safety. More gunfire came my way, but I was not hit. Denny was immediately transported to the hospital.

The doctors were able to keep Denny alive long enough so that his family and friends could see him once more and say good-bye. Even though Denny remained unconscious, his soul was still in the room. You could feel his presence before they turned off the life-support.

I'll never know what inspired me to answer this call for backup—but I can live the rest of my life knowing I helped a fellow officer get his last wish.

A Sheepdog's Duty

Kayla's bulging file lay on an already cluttered office desk, surrounded by student absence slips, class schedules, and two empty Styrofoam cups. Kayla was about to begin classes at Clare Middle School. She was twelve years old and in the seventh grade.

The thumbnail photographs in her file depicted a happy child. Each image was of a little girl with blonde hair, blue eyes, and a crooked smile mugging for the camera. From kindergarten to seventh grade, only her gradual maturation showed—the eyes and smile remained the same. The large amount of paperwork the file contained was because Kayla was continuously moving. Her seven years of education took place in seventeen different schools.

I ask the principals of each of my schools to notify me whenever we have a new student. I always meet with the child on his or her first day to introduce myself and explain what I do as a police school liaison officer. I offer the new students help in any way that I can and let them know how they can contact me.

Kayla burst through the office door like she had attended the school for years. The two secretaries paused in their duties, a parent dropping off a student's forgotten lunch money stared, and I put aside my normally reserved first-meeting face and did my best to stifle a laugh.

Kayla was a G.L.K. The acronym in the Clare educational system means "Goofy Looking Kid." Her dirty blonde hair was piled high in 1970's fashion and held in place with a large plastic clip that seemed more suited for a bag of potato chips. Hanging from her ears and around her neck was an abnormally large

104

and gaudy set of plastic costume-jewelry. Kayla wore a low-cut flowered sundress, six-inch black high-heeled shoes that were at least three sizes too big, and a dirty-brown canvas jacket. When she walked across the terrazzo floor, she sounded like a Clydesdale on pavement and looked like a prepubescent version of the character Mrs. Wiggins from the Carol Burnett show.

She'll never survive, I thought. The idea that in a few minutes this G.L.K. would be walking into a junior-high classroom brought only one conclusion: they'll tear her apart! Kayla walked up to me and offered her hand.

"My name is Kayla," she said. "Are you the principal?" I told her who I was and what I did and a little about the school. Then I offered to walk her to class. She said okay and walked behind me in silence up the stairs to her classroom. Kayla was reaching for the door when I called to her.

"Kayla," I said, taking a moment to choose my words carefully. "If there is anything that you need help with, anything at all, you can always talk to me."

Kayla tilted her head and gave me a silly-boy glance. "I'll be fine, Mr. White. Don't worry about a thing. I really am fine!" She gave me another quick smile and walked confidently into the classroom.

As I walked back downstairs, I was overcome with the feeling that there really was something special about Kayla. And I was right. Eventually, Kayla would change my life.

It had been two days—two days of worrying about Kayla and wondering why I worried about her so much. The emails from her teachers telling me that she was doing fine did nothing to placate me.

I wanted to check on her. The bell rang for a change of classes and the hallways filled in seconds with adolescent motion. I actually heard Kayla before seeing her. It was the clomp, clomp, clomp of those oversized high heels on the terrazzo floor. "Hi,

Mr. White!" Kayla shouted from twenty feet away. She smiled and walked to me, still wearing the same flowered sundress, gaudy jewelry, and dirty tan coat.

"I just wanted to check on you," I said. "How are you doing?" I looked at her eyes, searching for any sign of trouble.

"You don't have to worry about me, Mr. White! I am doing fine. Promise!"

I looked at the throng of students milling around us. Kayla sensed my fear. "I really am doing fine," she said. "I like this school and I am making friends!"

I looked back at her eyes. "Remember, anytime you need anything, just call. OK?"

Kayla gave her signature grin. "I know, Mr. White. You told me on my first day. Remember?" Kayla shook her head and headed off to her next class. I left the middle school, no more relieved than when I first arrived.

For the next two months, I would check on Kayla once or twice a week. Each time she would clomp up to me in those oversized shoes and wearing that same, but always clean, flowered sundress. She would say she was fine and not to worry. Each time I would tell her to contact me if she needed anything.

By the end of March, I did not need to say anything to Kayla because she'd just walk up and say, "I'm doing fine, Mr. White!" In April, I decided that she really was doing okay and discontinued my biweekly visits, although I would run into her occasionally.

Another month passed since I last checked on her. It was late in the afternoon and I decided to see her before I left for the day. When I heard Kayla clomping towards me in the hallway, she smiled and seemed more upbeat than usual.

"Mr. White!" she nearly screamed as she walked up. Before I could respond, she reached into her purse and pulled out a folded piece of notebook paper. "Here," she said. "I wrote you a note. I colored the front myself!"

The front of the note was indeed decorative. My name was written in bold hollow script that was intricately colored with a series of gel pens. I thanked Kayla for the note and she clomped off down the hall. A school staff member came up and we began talking. I put the note in my coat pocket while we were talking and left the school shortly thereafter.

I was going on a fishing trip to my favorite trout stream. Trout camp. Spending the weekend with friends is what filled my mind as I drove home that afternoon. After a busy week in the school, it was nice to think about fishing and great times around a campfire.

A couple miles from my home is a railroad crossing. The line of already waiting cars frustrated me as I stopped and tried to hurry the train. It was while sitting there, anxious and frustrated that my departure was being delayed, that I remembered Kayla's note and cursed myself for having forgotten about it. As I pulled out the note, I took a brief moment to enjoy the wide mix of colors and appreciate the time she took to draw this for me. I opened the note and began to read:

> *Dear Mr. White,*
>
> *Hay, what'z sup? Not much here, just writing you a letter about me getting raped by my mom's boyfriend. It started 3 years ago at our house in Carrollton. He would wait till my mom was gone or was asleep.*
>
> *Then he would have me have sex with him. He would make me lay in the bed and take off my pants and shirt and then he would eat me out. When I tried to make him quit he wouldn't. The last time was Tuesday. He took me to the store to get a pop and candy bar. He got me a root beer & two king-size NutRageous and then took me to the park by the river. He drank one beer after the other. He told me that since I liked the song "Back Your Ass Up", to back my ass up, and then he made me have sex with him.*
>
> *The End.*
>
> *Love Kayla*

The car behind me honked as I put my truck in reverse and tried to move out of the line of cars. I worked my way around traffic and raced back to the police department. You could see my tire tracks on the pavement for almost six months after that day. I worked all night and did not go home until the man that violated Kayla was in jail.

Kayla moved again at the end of the school year. I never heard from her again.

I am now known as "Sheepdog." And it is because of this little girl, who until meeting me did not trust anyone with her pain, that I decided to dedicate my career to helping the victims of child sexual abuse.

Kayla forever changed my life.

An excerpt from the book *Promise Not to Tell*, by Alan L. White. For more information, visit: www.alanlwhite.com.

My Day in Court

It was an ordinary morning at the State Police Post in Bridgeport, Michigan. I was just getting ready to go for a lunch break with Bill Estlack, the court officer at the time, when Central Dispatch sent out a request for officers regarding a possible suicide. Bill and I decided to respond to the incident since we were nearby.

Dispatch advised that a distressed subject by the name of Allen had left a message on a friend's answering machine stating he wanted to kill himself. Allen's friend was concerned for Allen's safety. Allen could not work anymore due to a serious back injury and was apparently severely depressed about it.

When Bill and I arrived at an old dilapidated farmhouse, everything appeared quiet and serene. There were no vehicles parked outside, so we peered through one small opening on a garage window. Like many rundown residential buildings I'd visited, its windows were covered up in paper. We saw a pickup truck was parked inside.

Since there was a vehicle, we assumed someone was home. We knocked repeatedly on the front door, but got no answer. Since the call we were responding to was a safety/welfare check, we had no choice but to enter the house. It is always uncomfortable going into a stranger's house without receiving permission first. In this case, however, a man's life might be in danger, so we let ourselves in.

We checked all the rooms in the house and both of us called out Allen's name. "Allen, are you in here? Allen, where are you?"

There was no response.

I noticed a door that was cut into the corner of two walls. At first it looked like a closet, because the door was locked with a simple clasp; but when we opened the door a couple inches and looked inside, it was actually a bedroom. We could see the soles of a man's bare feet on the bed.

We said, "Allen, are you okay? Can we come in? We are state police troopers. We want to help you." As the door opened wider, we could see he had a gun.

I said, "Bill, he's got a gun! Don't go in there!"

Allen, who was half-dressed, sprawled out on the bed, and gripping a gun tightly in his left hand, yelled, "Go away! If you don't get out of my house, I'll stick this gun in my mouth and blow my head off!" Clearly, he was angry and in distress. What we didn't know was that Allen had also taken a bottle of pills, which were perhaps impairing his judgment. He was slurring his words and moving erratically, so both of us knew something wasn't right.

Allen climbed out of bed, stood up, and staggered to the door. He was flailing his pistol as he walked. I can barely describe what this man looked like now because all I remember is looking straight down the barrel of his pistol, which looked like the opening of a canon to me!

As he stumbled toward us, he kept yelling, "Get out of my house! This is my house. I don't want you here! I'm going to kill myself, and if you don't get out I will kill you first!" He seemed serious.

Initially Bill and I tried to find a safe place to retreat to inside the house, but it was too small and cramped. There was no room for any safe cover. There were piles of clothes and junk everywhere—but nothing that could guard against a bullet.

Even though we had every right to shoot Allen, since he pointed his handgun directly at us, both of us resisted shooting. We did not want to hurt him. Even though our guns were drawn in defense, we had come to save him. Bill and I made our way to the door and ran outside.

I believe Allen wanted us to kill him, and it did seem like a case where deadly force was justified. We were in danger. At the same time, though, we also knew this man was mentally ill and probably in terrible pain.

The emergency support team responded quickly to assist us, and eventually they talked Allen out of the house. At one point, however, Allen shot toward an assisting officer concealed behind the barn, who was covering the rear of the house. Bill and I were securing the front of the house while hiding behind a large oak tree. He said, "That man took a shot at me! Can you believe it?" I was glad he wasn't hurt, but also that *my* tree was big enough for three people!

Ultimately, Allen was arrested for felonious assault on a police officer and escorted to the county jail.

When it came for his trial, both my partner and I were subpoenaed. I was one of the last witnesses called to the stand. I was only a two-year trooper, naïve, and this was my first time testifying at an actual circuit court trial. The defense attorney badgered me on the stand. He asked, "Well, if my client really assaulted you and pointed his handgun at you, why the heck didn't you shoot him?" I sat there for a moment, shocked at the question.

He added, "Aren't you a trained killer? Trained to shoot anyone who puts you in danger? Aren't you trained to shoot when a gun is pointed at you? If my client *really* pointed his weapon at you and was so dangerous, then why didn't you shoot your gun?"

It should be noted that in this type of an assault case, the prosecution has to prove to a jury, beyond a shadow of doubt, that this man did, in fact, point his weapon and threaten to kill us both. I knew Allen had pointed the gun at each of us, and I still remembered the "canon" pointed directly at my face! Nevertheless, neither one of us had chosen to shoot him.

I looked at the defense attorney, still in disbelief that he had asked such a question, and replied humbly, "I- I didn't take this job to shoot anybody!" You could have heard a pin drop inside the courtroom. Then I looked at the jury. I said, "My job is not to shoot people. I took this job to help people. My job was to save this man's life!"

Allen was convicted of felonious assault. And after seventeen years in the police business, I have never hurt or killed anybody.

I pray I never will.

The Little Boy

I was the first police officer at the scene of a one-car accident, arriving only minutes after it happened. Except for my red patrol lights going round and round, the road was dark and lonely. It was the middle of the night. Whoever had called in this accident was nowhere to be seen.

A woman had rolled her SUV and was smashed between the driver's seat and steering wheel. She was dead. The silence gave a false sense of peace—until I heard the whimpering of a child.

I walked around the vehicle, which was lying on its side, and saw a little boy lying underneath it. The roof covered and pinned half his body, while his head and arms were free. I was alarmed. There was no way I could lift that vehicle! I phoned to make sure help was coming. I prayed that just one car with a bunch of people in it would drive by. But nobody came.

The child was conscious and in a surprised voice asked, "Are you a *real* state trooper?"

I chuckled, "Of course I am, silly! I know, I'm just a girl, huh?"

The boy gave a half-smile and then blurted out, "I want my mom! Where is my mom?" Suddenly marble-sized tears fell down his cheeks. I saw no reason to tell him that his mother had died. Instead, I tried to reassure him.

"My friends are helping her. They're going to take her to the hospital. But, you know what? I don't have any children. Could I be your mom just for a while?"

He nodded his head and said, "Okay . . ."

I took his hand in mine.

He was a sweet-faced boy with brown, curly locks. He had

113

the most beautiful, big eyes I'd ever seen. He looked up at me seriously. "Am I going to die?" he asked.

For a split second, I choked. He had obvious internal bleeding; things didn't look too good.

I regained my composure and without hesitation said, "No, you won't die. You know, whether you decide to live in Heaven, or if you choose to stay right here on earth, either way . . . you will still be you, and you will still be alive. Nobody ever dies. We all live forever."

He looked into my eyes and I felt that he understood.

With the hint of a smile, he squeezed my hand in trust. After what seemed like an eternal moment, he took his last breath and gently passed away.

Public to the Rescue

During my first few years as a female trooper (those young, ferocious years when you think you can do anything and want to prove yourself), I'm working in Bridgeport, Michigan. There is a popular landmark there known as the Zilwaukee Bridge, which extends over the Saginaw River. The bridge is very tall.

The "Z", as we call it, was undergoing construction. A large heavy sign has blown onto the roadway. Vehicles slow down, dodge the sign, and then speed up. I am certain it will cause an accident.

I exit my car and refuse to look down because I am afraid of heights. Although I'm only five feet, three inches tall, I decide I can move this eight-foot sign—by myself. The sign is cockeyed and lies slanted over a concrete median. Even though I can lift it only partially, and know it is really too heavy, I am determined to move it myself. I don't want to ask any male troopers for backup. I don't want to be judged a "helpless female." (I realize now how silly I was—a male trooper would certainly have called for assistance.)

Some cars have stopped before the sign, and others are going around it. I try valiantly to stand up the sign—not that I know what I'm going to do with it next.

I actually have the sign almost erect when suddenly a huge gust of wind sweeps across the bridge! I totally lose control of the sign. It blows and topples backwards, way too heavy for me to stop. I am sent spiraling on my ass!

Then the sign flounders and bangs on top of me and hits me square on the forehead! I'm not hurt, but I lie there motionless, because I'm too embarrassed to get up. I'm so embarrassed; I decide to stay underneath the sign! I pray, "Oh, please. Oh, please. Oh, please, God. Don't send anyone over to help me. Just let me lie here. I'd rather DIE than be helped!" I'm thinking, *Okay, nobody saw me. It's okay, nobody saw me. I'll just hide here for a little while longer and . . .*

But I soon hear the voices of public citizens—the battalion has arrived!

"Are you okay, Trooper? Are you okay? Here, let us get this sign off you! "

Here I am, a Michigan State Police trooper in fancy dress uniform with a noggin on my forehead and the biggest bruised ego you'd ever want to see. As I find my way, clumsily, from underneath the sign, I struggle to my feet. I am a bit confused and actually see a few stars. I can feel a huge round lump on my head the size of a golf ball.

"Oh, I'm fine. Really, I am," I say as I stumble (with citizen support no less) to my vehicle.

"Are you sure, Trooper? Are you sure?"

I nod in reply, totally embarrassed, as other citizens trail behind me like I'm the Pied Piper. To make matters worse, they seat me in my car and they go do MY JOB! They move the sign to its final resting place.

My humiliation is not yet over. My partner, Jerry, hears about the incident (partners are ruthless) and he contacts the media. He tells the media *everything* that happened! Oh, yeah—he makes the story good and juicy, too, as detailed as possible. He finishes by saying, ". . . and if it wasn't for those brave Michigan citizens, Trooper Bentley might still be under that sign today. Those citizens should be very proud of a job well done!" You have to be around the media to know how much they really dig this type of "human interest" story.

Later that night, I turn on the TV. There they all are . . . reporters at the Zilwaukee Bridge, focusing their cameras on the cockamamie sign! I am at home by myself, listening, growing more and more mortified, as my face gets hotter and hotter. *Then I see my face on TV—a close-up no less!* The reporter finishes his story, stating ". . . and thank goodness Trooper Bentley only suffered a minor abrasion to the forehead and was able to work the rest of her shift. Who knows what could have happened if concerned citizens hadn't helped her along."

Oh Ye of Little Faith

I was on patrol when a 911 went out about a person hit by a car. A ten-year-old girl had been hit by a pick-up truck traveling sixty-five miles an hour. When I arrived on the scene, she looked like a full-grown adult because her body was so swollen. Both arms and legs were broken and turned in the wrong direction. I had to adjust her head three different times to keep her breathing.

She and her sister had been running down the side of the road to meet their father, who was plowing a nearby field on his tractor. The victim ran ahead of her sister and was turning around in the road to run back to her sister, when she was hit. Unfortunately, her sister saw it happen. The father was now at the scene.

We had the girl air-lifted to Detroit Children's Hospital. Since it was the end of my shift, I didn't phone the hospital for an update until the next day. I was certain the case was a fatal accident.

The hospital spokesperson would not give me the list of injuries, even though I was the investigating officer. I explained I already knew she had two broken arms and legs. "I'm sorry. You don't understand. It is not that we *won't* give you this information, we just *can't*. All I can tell you is that she has spent eighteen hours in brain surgery and it looks like she's going to live."

I said, "So what does that mean?"

The nurse said, "She's probably going to be a vegetable; but it looks like she is going to live."

I thought to myself, *Oh God! Why didn't you just take this ten-year-old girl, instead of letting her live the rest of her life as a vegetable?* It upset me. I reflected on this for awhile, then let go of the matter entirely—at least I thought I did.

About six months later I was giving a career day talk at Brown City Elementary School, when a girl came up to me. "You don't remember me, do you?" she said.

I said, "No."

She said, "You were there, when my sister got hit by the truck."

My heart sunk deep into my chest. I realized I hadn't let go of the issue, really. I didn't know what to say, so I asked, "How is she?"

"She's doing great!" the girl answered. "Sometimes she forgets what happened a long time ago, and sometimes her left arm goes numb, but she is almost ready to come back to school! You should stop by our house because my parents would really like to thank you."

When I heard this, I thought, *Oh, ye of little faith*. My faith in God was restored. And I was reminded that I became a trooper to save lives and that I do make a difference in the world.

Three Dogs

A few years ago, when I was in police uniform, I visited the local Humane Society. I was interested in getting a dog for companionship as I had recently gone through a divorce and a work transfer. As I looked at the dogs, I thought to myself, I'll adopt the first dog that comes up to me.

As I wandered past the cages, I noticed a small shaggy mutt laboriously walk up to the bars of its cell and look at me. I thought, I know he is the first dog to come up to me, but I was hoping for a bigger dog, a more manly dog. I wasn't ready to commit, so I decided to think about it over night and return the next day.

I decided to get the dog. However, the following afternoon, when I returned to the Humane Society, I couldn't find the dog. I thought, Good, somebody took him home! I went up to the lady to inquire. "I wanted that little dog that walked up to me yesterday. I thought he chose me as an owner. But I see someone has already taken him home."

Remembering me from yesterday, she shook her head forlornly. "I'm sorry, officer, but we put him to sleep this morning. He wasn't well. He had kennel cough and we couldn't afford to give him medicine or medical care. I'm sorry. I didn't know you were interested in him."

I was devastated to learn that the dog was euthanized because of my hesitation. I didn't mean for this to happen. Streams of guilt and sadness reared their ugly heads. While still trying to recover from this unexpected shock, I looked at the other dogs. Somehow, today, the more manly dogs were no longer attractive to me.

Then I noticed another small dog that must have arrived

today. I know I didn't see him yesterday. I could tell he was old and blind. He looked sad—kind of like me at the moment. He was curled up in the corner of his cell. He raised his head once and seemingly looked at me, but I doubt he saw me; his eyes were so milky.

The attendant shook her head in disgust, "Officer, it should be criminal what that family did. They owned that dog for seventeen years and then just gave it up to the Humane Society. Apparently they were moving. What were they thinking? How can people do that to an old, faithful animal? They should go to jail! It's just wrong. Nobody will ever take an elderly dog like that and he won't last much longer."

My chest thumped in discomfort as I compassionately looked at the old dog. I was trying to determine the practicality of adopting him. It was impractical; the dog would need medical care. And, it couldn't see well. And, I also had the added stress of paying child support each week. All of these issues weighed heavily on my mind. The thought of bringing him home was out of the question.

The dog looked at me again and then gave up. He put his head down as if to say, "Just go away. I'm may be old but I have dignity!"

Then a very old man with a cane walked through the door. He moved slowly and carefully. He saw the dog instantly. The dog looked up at the old man, but then put his chin back down. It was as if the dog said, "Oh what's the use? Just forget it! I'm too old, crippled, and blind. Don't look at me like some freak in a circus. Why would you ever want someone like me? Go away! I know you won't take me either." Then the dog closed his eyes and shivered like old men do.

Without hesitation, the old man said, "I'll get that old dog."

My heart stopped—as if telling me, "See, dumb dumb! The old man listened to his heart and responded. Why didn't you? I am so much bigger and more intelligent than the practicality of your brain!"

The attendant said to the old man, "But, sir, I must warn you, he is a very old dog, blind, has arthritis, and needs shots. He . . ." Her voice trailed off as I watched the old man shuffle up to the locked gate.

He spoke as if he had not heard a word she said. "I don't care about that. I want to get the damn dog! Look, he's all alone . . ."

She unlocked the gate. The old man hobbled past the gate to the dog, which now stood up on all fours with some difficulty. The man insisted on picking up the dog. Briefly setting aside his cane, he managed to lift the dog with both arms. He said, "Hey there, old feller, your family died, too, didn't they?" The little dog lay his head on the man's chest, as if to say "Thank, God, someone came to get me. I'm going home now."

As he carefully walked out the door, I heard him mumble to the dog, "Come on, old feller, we can grow old and die together— even if we only have a few months."

I was ashamed of myself and vowed I would somehow make up for these mistakes. I saw that the language of the heart seemed far superior to the practicality of my head and that the old man and the dogs had taught me something.

Two years went by. I never did get a dog and had voluntarily transferred to a police post five hundred miles north. It was bitter cold during the winter but Lake Superior and the land were beautiful. So, one day I parked my patrol car near the bay. As I ate a stale homemade sandwich for lunch I watched the water lapping over the edge of the ice, which sometimes extended two to three hundred yards out. The wind was blistery and treacherous that day, kicking up the fluffy snow on the portions of the bay that were iced over.

As I was eating, I saw a few people congregating to my left.

They were looking out over the bay and I wondered what they were peering at. I turned my car off and got out. I heard the most pitiful, ear-wrenching, animal cry for help that I ever did hear. In the distance, on the ice, was a small dog.

I walked up to the group of people, all bundled up in their winter attire, but none willing to go out on the ice. One said, "We don't know whose dog that is, but we think it is stuck in the ice. We don't know how long it has been out there; we don't think he'll last much longer."

I heard the horrible howling cry from the dog again and couldn't take it anymore. I said, "I'll get that old dog," and started back to the patrol car. One of the bystanders said, "But, officer, the ice is really dangerous right now! Notice there are no ice shanties on the bay. You could fall through the ice ..."

I interrupted, "I don't care about that. I want to get the darn dog. Look, he's all alone out there." I retrieved my snowshoes from the trunk and put them on. The snowshoes were not required patrol car equipment but I was glad I packed them. I also grabbed a shovel, just in case.

The snow and ice creaked under my snowshoes as I slowly shuffled my way to the dog. It appeared the dog had now lain down. I thought, At least the snowshoes are wider and bigger than my feet and seem to be distributing my weight better over this ice. The ice was, indeed, pretty thin. It was being insulated from the snow lying on top. I walked slowly and carefully to the dog.

After what seemed like forever, I finally reached him. I looked over the dog carefully. It appeared harmless and its eyes were closed. It was shivering, so I knew it was still alive. One foot appeared stuck in the ice. I started feeling déjà vu. I thought, Have I been through something like this before? The dog looked up at me but didn't seem to see me.

It was obvious the dog was in shock. It must have been out

here a long time, especially for the ice to freeze around its foot. I broke away the ice with my shovel and freed the dog's foot, then carefully picked him up, and placed him inside my jacket. I said, "Hey there, old feller, where did your family go? Did they abandon you?"

The little dog laid his head on my chest, exhausted, as if to say, "Thank God, someone came to get me. I'm finally going home!"

Slowly and carefully, I walked back to the car, knowing that we could still fall through the ice. I hoped that the dog was going to live.

As I lay the dog gently inside the patrol car, I remembered the old man at the Humane Society, from two years ago. "Come on, old feller," I said, "maybe we can grow old and die together— even if we only have a few more minutes."

Fortunately, the dog made a complete recovery.

Nobody ever claimed the dog.

Symbols, Signs & Synchronicity

In police investigations, symbols, signs, and synchronicity play similar roles, turning up much-needed information through sources not otherwise available. Carl Jung's theory of synchronicity states that events widely separated in time and space cannot possibly come together by simple coincidence but must be guided by another power. Whether one is a Carl Jung enthusiast or not, most police officers would agree that there is a peculiar gray line between pure coincidence and divine intervention.

"Chance favors the prepared mind."

Louis Pasteur

"There is no such thing as chance; and what seem to us merest accident springs from the deepest source of destiny."

Friedrich Schiller

The Grim Reaper

The Rookie – Part 1

My first Saturday night-fourth day on the job. "Car number six," crackled the radio, "we have a report of a cutting at 765 Margaret. Advise on an ambulance."

"Car number six, okay," I responded.

I pulled my brand-new black leather gloves off the dash and put them on. Then I reached into the backseat and grabbed my nightstick. "Do you want me to turn on the siren?" I excitedly asked John.

"No! Hell no!" he laughed. He had an easy, natural laugh. "There will be plenty of crazies there without us calling more in." John casually grabbed his coffee off the dashboard while I sat beside him with my helmet and gloves on. I had my night stick in my hands, ready, although I didn't know what for.

John was a former Marine drill instructor and a veteran police officer. He had been in the trenches and was worn and battle-scarred. John was missing part of his right hand. I heard someone shot it off with a shotgun. I never heard the whole story. I never asked John about it either. I learned early on that you don't talk about such things and that cops are taught to never look back.

I liked John. He was smart. Someone said he had been through law school and had passed the state bar exam. He could have been an attorney but opted to remain a cop. He requested duty in the ghetto. No one asked him why.

John finished his coffee, threw the paper cup in the backseat, and we drove to Margaret Street. My first big call—I didn't know whether to take my helmet off or leave it on. Rookie lesson number one: always wait until your partner puts on his helmet before you put on yours.

When we arrived, we met a big brawny black woman. She was naked and her arms were covered with droplets of blood where she had been cut in various places. She left a trail of red wherever she went. John called her by name. Wanda.

Wanda was pissed off but not the least bit concerned about her nudity. I'll always remember the stretch marks on her body. She was battle worn and rough.

We found a white male in the bedroom, also naked. He was bloody but not from being cut. It was Wanda's blood. The man was glad to see us. Wanda had kicked his butt!

I didn't know what to do. I was trying to act cool, like this was nothing new to me. I had spent the last four years in an ivy-covered building at Michigan State University. They hadn't taught me anything about this.

John and Wanda were walking around and talking to each other, like they were good friends. They acted like nothing was out of the ordinary. Wicked Wanda, her nickname, was still completely naked. Every minute or so she would casually wipe blood off her arms. John finally asked her if she wanted an ambulance. She refused.

The man in the bedroom accused Wanda of stealing his wallet. Wanda denied it. She accused him of cutting her up. The man said nothing. I realized that Wanda and John were looking for the man's clothes. I found his pants behind a rickety old chair in the living room. I picked them up and felt something in a pocket. It was his wallet. When Wanda saw the wallet, she pushed past John and attacked the man again!

He was no match for her. He tried to defend himself but was not doing a very good job of it. John just let her go. I was totally confused. It seemed liked we should have been doing something other than standing by and letting Wanda kick this guy all over the bedroom.

Finally she stopped, satisfied with her effort. She walked

around the small apartment picking up her clothes. Once she had all her things in a big wad under her arm she walked right out the front door and down the street, naked as the day she was born.

The man quickly put on his pants and shirt. He asked if he was going to jail. John casually answered, "No." I don't know who was more surprised, me or the man. I was sure someone would be going to jail. The man left in a hurry, without his shoes, not taking a chance that John might change his mind.

I found one of his shoes under the coffee table. John told me to pick up the shoe and find the second one. I did. "What are we going to do with the shoes?" I asked.

John answered, "Tomorrow's Sunday. It should be a slow day. Let's take them to the man's house and return them. That will give him something to think about. Let him explain it to his wife!"

"He was married?" I asked.

"He had on a wedding ring," answered John. "I'm guessing he's not homosexual if he's jumping Wanda's bones."

John taught me a lot. He taught me how to survive and how to stay alive. We became good friends. I told myself that if I ever became a veteran officer, I too, would teach recruits as much as I could. John was a great teacher and I loved his easy, natural laugh.

The Veteran – Part 2

May 28th, 11:25 P.M. I had paid my dues for twenty years in the big city and had scars to show. Thirty-five minutes left on my shift. It had been a long night—unseasonably warm. Someone said it was 85 degrees when we started work this afternoon. Must still be in the mid- to high seventies. My assignment tonight was accident investigator for the North End. Jerry and I were the only accident investigators on the street that night. We had both been busy. I saw him in the station around 8:30 P.M. He had investigated five accidents to my seven. I was up to nine accidents now.

I had just left a restaurant where I had a coffee and finished several accident reports. It was 10:30 P.M. before I had an opportunity to stop and take a break. I was past being hungry, so I didn't eat. Two middle-aged women sat in the booth directly behind me. They were discussing death. The older woman was about forty-five, weathered, worn, and wearing clothes that were not color-coordinated. She must have had a son in the service. Her argument was how terrible it would be to lose a son at war, to have him shot and dying in the battlefield. The younger woman, about thirty-six, well-dressed and attractive, countered, "It would be terrible to lose a son or any child, even if they died in a hospital."

The older woman rebutted, "At least in a hospital you could hold your child as he or she died. On the battlefield, they die alone."

I thought about that and agreed with her. I have four kids and never thought about them dying. The older lady was right. No one, especially a child, should have to die and face the Grim Reaper alone.

I was stopped at a red light on Fifth Avenue, eastbound at Martin Luther King, debating which way to go. The light turned green, I turned left and went back into the inner city. I doubled-back to Dupont Street and proceeded north. When I crossed Stewart Avenue, I saw something ahead and to the right, just off the road. Something was wrong. I couldn't see for sure what it was. Smoke or dust filled the air. It was a car upside-down, resting on its roof; it had smashed into a telephone pole. I pulled up and turned on my emergency lights.

The dispatcher crackled, "Are you still North? Need you to check a rollover accident. Possible fatal."

I reached over and keyed the mike, "If you are referring to Dupont, north of Stewart, I'm on location."

"Your time is 11:47 P.," he answered. Then he asked, "Any car North to assist #71?" No one replied. Everyone was in for a shift change. I was the only car in the north end. I was on my own.

I found a male black subject—no, it was a female subject—with short hair. She was wearing a long red dress. On my third look, I determined, no, it was a black male in a long red dress. He was crushed behind the steering wheel. If he was not dead, he should have been from the looks of the car.

I had to lie down on the street to get a good look. The driver was the only person in the car. Definitely male. He reeked of alcohol. "Hey there! Hey!" I shouted. There was no response. I reached around his neck with my left hand to see if I could find a pulse or any trace of life. Nothing.

He was wearing a thin, yellow, nylon cord and a string of beads around his neck. With what kids were wearing today, neither of these seemed out of the ordinary. Suddenly it dawned on me, however. One of the area high schools had graduated their senior class tonight. This young kid had graduated today. He was wearing his graduation gown.

I went to my car to notify dispatch that I had a possible fatal accident and to request an ambulance, the rescue squad, and two additional units to help with measurements and crowd control. A large crowd was starting to gather.

I returned to the wrecked car. I thought I heard a moan. I reached back in. I still couldn't feel a pulse. Then he moved slightly. "Am I going to die, mister? I don't want to die!" he said. The boy was frightened. I couldn't believe he was alive.

"Hang on, man. I've got you," I said. "You just lay cool. I've got help coming. Try not to move. They will be here in a minute." I then asked, "How much liquor have you had to drink tonight?" If he lived, I needed a statement, an admission, for the accident report.

"I was just seeing if this car could fly," he stated. He laughed as he spoke. He had a natural, easy smile. WHAM!!! A piece of cement or asphalt crashed into the side of the car. Some jerk threw it at me.

"Someone's lookin' to get his butt kicked," I said. The kid laughed, easily and naturally.

"Don't leave me, okay?" he pleaded.

"I'm right here. I've got you. When I get you out of here, though, I'm taking you to jail for being stupid and trying to fly a car," I said.

The kid laughed again. Like it was a part of his speech.

I heard the coarse, raspy voice for the first time. "I saw it! I saw the whole thing!" it shouted. "The cop was chasing him and done ran him off the road and into that pole!" This jerk was my last concern. Right now I was trying to figure out how to keep this boy alive until help arrived.

A rock came flying by my head, about two feet to the left. It hammered into the side of the car. I had to ignore it. This boy needed to get to a hospital. I raised up on my knees and grabbed the portable radio attached to my belt. "I need some help up here! My driver is still alive. See if you can scramble the rescue squad." Radio didn't answer.

"Mister, don't leave me, don't leave me." It sounded like his voice was getting stronger. I lay back down next to the window.

"I'm here, man," I said. "You're going to be all right. The fire department should be rolling up any second now."

"Fire department?" the kid questioned.

I answered, "Yeah, just in case your butt catches on fire, they'll put it out for you." We both laughed.

The kid put his hand on my arm. "What's your name?"

"I'm Mike. Mike Thomas," I answered. "You can call me Mike if you want. You got a name?"

The kid smiled. "Yeah, I'm Johnny. Johnny Johnson. You can call me Johnny if you want."

Johnny Johnson from years ago, I remembered. What was

it, ten, twelve years? I had lost track. "Would you be Johnny Johnson, the little frickin' bike thief?" I laughed.

Johnny laughed, too. "Hey! I want to know how you knew that. How did you know I stole that damn bike?"

"I'm a dad, man," I said. "Dads know stuff like that, it's what dads do."

"Oh. I never had a dad, Mike."

I didn't respond.

"I'm going to die, Mike! I know I'm going to die!" Johnny said.

"You're not going to die, man," I assured him. "You ain't going to be dancing for awhile, I can tell you that. You've got one leg that is pointing in a strange direction; but don't worry . . . I'm not going to let you die. I've got you."

I felt the beads around his neck. "What's all this?"

"The cord is for being the salutatorian of my class," he laughed, in his easy natural way. "The necklace is something Mrs. Kah, my English teacher, gave me. It's called a rose or something like that. She said I was special," and then Johnny laughed again. He added, "Special, my black butt. She gave me a C in Advanced English Composition and knocked my straight four-point grade average right in the frickin' head."

I pulled the beads out from under his gown. "This is a rosary!" I said. "She gave you a rosary for graduation? Are you Catholic?"

"That's it," Johnny said. "That's the word—it's a rosary. I thought she called it a rose. What do you do with it? What's it for?"

A barrage of rocks and cement came crashing in on me and the side of the car. They didn't hurt. They pissed me off more than anything. I heard the raspy voice again. He was shouting something stupid. That son-of-a-bitch might as well give his soul to Jesus, I thought, because his butt is going to belong to me!

"You use a rosary to pray. Some people say the rosary when

they pray for something special," I answered. "You're not Catholic, are you?"

"No, I ain't nothin' as far as church goes. I don't go to church."

"The rescue squad is coming out of Station #8," crackled the radio. "They are en route." I acknowledged by clicking my radio mike twice.

I liked this kid. He would make a good cop. He was black, bright, and witty. I would make it a point to follow up with him this summer. I would encourage him to become a Man in Blue or Brown. Another rock bounced off the street and hit my leather gun belt. Didn't hurt, but it was a direct hit. I heard the raspy voice laugh . . . a laugh I will always remember.

I reached for my radio, "I need some help up here. Get me some backup, please!"

After a short pause, the radio came on, "Rescue squad is en route, 71. I'll try and get someone out of roll call. Just hold what you've got—hang on." It was a new voice; they had changed dispatchers. Third shift patrol would be checking in soon.

I turned back to Johnny and said, "You picked a bad time to have an accident."

"Mike, tell me about the rosary. Do you know how to pray it?"

I pulled it out from around his head and showed him the beads. "Never wear it around your neck, man. You just hold it in your hands. You should have a little case to carry it in." Johnny nodded. "The way I do it is to say three Hail Mary's and then I pray for something. I'm a part-time farmer, so sometimes I pray for rain and sometimes I pray for it to stop raining." We both laughed. I could hear a siren way off in the distance. Help was coming. Several more rocks crashed down on us. Neither of us acknowledged them. "After you say the three Hail Mary's, you just keep going around the beads until you come back to here."

I pointed to where the chain came back around to the start. "When you reach the larger beads along the way, you say the Lord's Prayer."

"Teach me the prayer, Mike, will ya?" Johnny asked, as another rock bounced off the pavement and into my leg.

I took the beads in my hand and started to recite, "Hail Mary, full of grace, the Lord is with Thee. Blessed art thou among women and blessed is the fruit of thy womb Jesus. Hail Mary, Mother of God, pray for us sinners, now and at the hour of our death."

Johnny and I said it two more times together and then I added, "God, spare the life of this little bike thief."

Johnny laughed and said, "God, don't let the brothers hit my friend Mike in the head with a rock." We both had a good chuckle.

The raspy voice was heard again, along with another barrage of rocks and cement. This time one hit me square on the left shoulder blade. It hurt. "#$%!!" I yelled.

"It's sure funny, Mike," Johnny laughed. "You helping me like this, saying the rosary and all, and the brothers are chuckin' rocks at you."

I could hear several sirens now—sounded good. "Help's coming," I said. "Do you know who that guy is with the raspy voice? Do you know that voice?"

"Never heard it before," Johnny answered. "Never heard it before in my life. He's sure actin' a fool, though." I didn't know if Johnny was telling me the truth or not.

Sweat was running into my eyes. It was still hot and muggy, must have been in the high seventies. I pulled my arm out and looked at my watch. 12:17 A.M.

"Don't leave me, Mike! Don't leave me alone!" Johnny pleaded again. "I'm cold. I'm freezing," he said.

I reached around his side, under his arm and around his body.

I felt wetness, blood—lots of it. Johnny was hurt—more than I thought. His body was covered with blood. He just might die. I could see both of his legs were bent, twisted, and broken. Too much blood. He was in bad shape. I had thought he was getting stronger. Now, I knew differently.

A rock smashed into the back of my hand that was braced against the car. I heard the raspy voice shout, "Got the bastard! Got him on the hand." It laughed. He will pay the price for that, I thought. I will see that he does.

Johnny wasn't saying anything now. He was quiet. Bleeding to death. I couldn't do a thing to help him. I could only hold him, hold him and let him die. I felt strange lying there with my arm around Johnny. I couldn't leave him. I felt a strange responsibility to stay with him. It was a father's love for a son that kept me there. At that moment, I was Johnny's father and he was my son.

I also had a growing hate building up inside of me—an urge to beat the fool with the raspy voice, to beat him unconscious, and then just walk away. My blood was boiling with an overpowering love and an unquenchable hate. Johnny squeezed my arm one more time and then died in my arms.

I collected Johnny's personal things and headed for his house. It was 2:15 A.M. when I pulled up in front of the address on Johnny Johnson's driver's license. He lived on Margaret Street. Lights were still on in the house and I could hear a TV. I knocked on the door. No one answered. I knocked again.

"What the f— do you want?" came a gruff voice from inside.

"It's the police! Open up the door!" I ordered.

An old, hard-looking woman opened the door. "What do you want? What is it?" she asked.

We looked at each other and I said, "I need to talk to you. Can I come in?" The lady stepped back and left the door open. I followed her inside. I had seen this woman before but didn't know where. She had cold untrusting eyes. She was probably not as old as she looked.

"What did Johnny steal? What kind of trouble is he in now? Is he in jail?" she asked. I handed her the yellow nylon cord. She didn't take it. She knew. I laid it on the coffee table. She sat down, half falling into an old chair. I sat down on the couch which was equally worn. Neither of us said anything. There was nothing to say. I was going to tell her that Johnny was driving a stolen car—but why? She didn't care. I could have told her he had been drinking and was drunk—but who cares now? What difference does it make? I could have told her he was going 100 miles an hour, but I didn't. What would be the point? I wished I was telling her he was in jail for stealing a car, for reckless driving, and driving drunk. Instead, I was telling her that her son was dead.

I suddenly realized who she was and where I had seen her. She was Wicked Wanda, the prostitute who lived on Margaret Street. I didn't think she'd remember me—it had been almost twenty years.

Wanda broke the silence, "Is John still around? Do you have contact with him?"

"No," I answered, surprised by the questions. "John retired several years ago. I heard he moved up north someplace. I could probably contact him, though. Why do you ask?"

Wanda sighed. "Would you find him? He should know about Johnny. He would want to know."

The easy natural smile, the charismatic personality, the exceptional intelligence, the lighter complexion—suddenly, it all made sense. John, my old teacher and partner, was Johnny's father. "I will let him know, Wanda," I said. "Do you want me to ask him to call?"

"No," she answered, "just let him know about Johnny."

I got up and turned off the TV, and then Wanda and I talked

for over an hour. Simple conversation, broken up with long periods of calm silence. There was no hate. No fear. No racial attitudes. I asked her if Johnny had a friend with a raspy voice. She wanted to know why. She was street smart. "Oh, I need to talk to him about the accident," I lied. She told me that Johnny had many friends, but she didn't know of any with a raspy voice. I believed her. I would have to find the guy on my own.

I got up to leave. Wanda walked me to the door. "Was Johnny alone when he died?" she asked. I told her that I was with him, by his side. She seemed pleased.

I started home. In three weeks I would have twenty years on the job. Twenty years of busting heads, twenty years of giving people directions, twenty years of love and joy, twenty years of hate and grief. Twenty years of fighting and dying, laughing and crying. Twenty years of solving problems and twenty years of facing problems that simply have no solutions. Twenty years of refusing to back down, never apologizing, and never looking back.

The Grim Reaper – Part 3

I walked into the house around 4:30 A.M., too exhausted to even be tired. My shoulders and hips ached. Everything hurt. I kicked off my shoes, tossed my gun and gun belt on the sofa, pulled off my shirt and threw it over the back of the recliner. I made a trail from the back door to the refrigerator. I reached for a Coke, then put it back. I grabbed a beer. Then I grabbed another beer and opened them both. I took an old, insulted 32-ounce mug out of the cupboard and poured both beers into it. I walked back to the recliner, threw my uniform shirt on the floor, and sat down. I took a big drink of the ice-cold beer and leaned back. Something was in my pocket. It was the rosary—I still had Johnny's rosary—his "rose."

I touched the first bead. "Hail Mary, full of grace, the Lord is with Thee." That must have been where you were tonight, Lord. You must have been with Thee, because you sure weren't with me. 'Ol Johnny and I could have used a little help from you tonight, man. You could have covered my ass a little.

"Blessed art thou among women, and blessed is the fruit of thy womb Jesus." I wonder if Johnny knew what that meant, Jesus being the fruit of thy womb. Mary is the mother of Jesus. I should have explained that to him. He said he never went to church. I probably should have told him about that. Hell, I didn't think he was going to die! I wonder why the young and innocent die and the old farts like me keep on living? Just doesn't seem fair.

"Holy Mary, Mother of God, pray for us sinners, now and at the hour of our death." I prayed for Johnny and I prayed for Wanda. I tossed the rosary over to the sofa. I would take it back to Wanda tomorrow.

I finished the beers. It was starting to get light outside. I decided to go out and feed the steers—they would be surprised to see me this early in the morning. As I started down to the barn, it began to sprinkle. Thunder was rolling off to the south. I fed the steers and the other livestock and ran into the barn just before it started to rain. The rain was pounding on the steel roof.

I decided to make myself comfortable, so I sat down and put my feet up on some bags of bean seed. Oh, to be a kid again. Those were the days. Didn't have to worry about anything. I relaxed into my bean bag chair. It felt good; it smelled good. I thought about Johnny wearing the rosary around his neck. He thought it was a necklace. I laughed out loud, just me, the animals, and the rain on the roof. We sure live in a strange world. I laughed again. I laughed until I cried. Tears came to my eyes. I started to look back.

CHRIST! DON'T EVER LOOK BACK! I started to cry. I cried out every tear in my head. Twenty years of tears. Twenty

years of never backing down. Twenty years of never apologizing.
Twenty years of never looking back. I laughed. I cried.
  Finally, I slept.

The Grim Reaper slipped into my dreams.
Appeared in the rear of my barn.
I sat up with a start when he called me by name,
His gravely voice, his cold stare, his "Death" charm.

He's invaded my dreams many times in the past, but never spoken a word
Tonight he had something important to say, a message he thought must be
  heard.
He told me that Johnny's time had come, that it was his turn to go.
I put up a formidable fight, but he'd come to get Johnny's soul.

"God didn't abandon you, Mike, as you lay in the street all alone.
He needed you to turn loose your grip, so I could take Johnny home.
The decision was made to take Johnny back, the decision was made up
  above,
You held him as long as you could, my friend, with your faith, your
  caring, your Love."

The reaper then laughed, he laughed right out loud, a laugh I'll never
  forget.
It was the raspy voice from the accident scene, it stood the hair up on my
  neck.
"So, it was you along, you bastard, you ass, inciting the crowd with
  your chants.
I wanted to kill you," I said to his face, "I would have, if given the
  chance."

"It's my job, don't you see?" he said, as he laughed, "I must say it's a job
  that I dread.
"You cops just don't understand God's way, give up, let it go . . . Johnny's
  dead.

"You cops are all the same, I
might add, never back down,
apologize, or look back.
"But I know when you're frightened
and sad . . . .I know when you
re-live the past."

"My hood's off to you and to all
of you cops, all of you mortals
in Blue,
"I have to admit I admire your
style, because, I was once a
cop, too."
With that he laughed and just
faded away . . . it's his laugh
I'll remember the most . . .
The Grim Reaper had been a cop
in the past; the Grim Reaper
was a cop's ghost!

I awoke with a start. Was that a dream or did it really happen? The sun was out. It was 7:15 A.M. I had slept for two hours. As I walked back to the house, I saw my wife in the window. She waved, wondering where I'd been all night.

Michael Thomas, Retired
Flint Police Department

How Could this Possibly Happen?

Several years ago, when I was on patrol, I received a call for police assistance regarding a car/motorcycle crash. My partner and I responded to the location. When we arrived, we found a male subject lying face down in the ditch. It was the motorcyclist, who was pronounced dead at the scene.

We noticed the car with heavy damage to the passenger side door. The motorcyclist had come over a hill, just as the car was pulling into a driveway on the road. The motorcyclist was speeding. The driver of the car could not avoid the collision in time, and the motorcyclist hit the side of the car at full speed.

The driver was white as a ghost. He appeared to be in total shock. Shock is not rare in such a situation, but this man appeared to be in a trance. He stared blankly as he recalled what had happened.

He explained, "I'm from over 150 miles away from here. I drove north to meet my friend, at this house. I was just pulling into his driveway when the motorcycle hit me. We were planning a fishing trip to Canada. I haven't been here in a long time . . ."

The man was in "the Zone" and I wasn't about to interrupt him. I couldn't identify what his stare was all about, though. All I knew was that something was very wrong. It was as if he'd had his own near-death experience.

"When the motorcycle hit my car, I saw the man's body fly into the ditch. There wasn't anything I could have done to avoid it." He was shaking his head slowly as he spoke, as if I wasn't there. "I get out of my car, but suddenly I see my sister-in-law running down the road. She is screaming. She is running to the man in the ditch . . . my SISTER-IN-LAW!" The man hesitates.

"Officer, I thought it was a dream . . . I thought, how can this possibly be? My sister-in-law, she lives downstate, over a two-hour drive from here. I thought I was seeing a ghost. Then . . . it all suddenly dawned on me . . ." The man's voice trembles and trails off in silence, as I'm trying to comprehend what he is saying.

He sadly utters, "That was my brother on the motorcycle."

I said, "What?"

He continued, "I knew we each had a friend in this area, but we never knew each other's friends personally. We had no idea we'd both be here today. I haven't even seen my brother in quite some time, because we live so far apart from each other. I can't believe we're in this same town together! How could I be here just in time for him to hit me?"

I stood there, astonished, feeling great sadness for the man. As we sorted things out, I learned his brother was helping a friend repair his motorcycle. He was simply test riding his friend's motorcycle when the accident occurred. Neither brother knew they would see each other. What were the odds that a man kills his own brother in an accident so far away from both of their homes?

What were the odds that this could happen?

Karmic Happenings

Early one evening, I was patrolling alone and decided to stop a vehicle with its taillight out. As I walked up to the car, the male driver jumped out. He was noticeably upset.

"Please, officer. Don't arrest me! I'm suspended," he begged. "In fact, I'm *very suspended*. I don't have a license. I know there is a warrant out for me . . . *please* don't arrest me." He was actually shaking. I genuinely felt sorry for him, but cautiously directed him to return to his car.

I said, "Calm down. No matter what happens, everything will be okay. Be seated in your car and let me run your name through the computer. Let me see what is going on for you."

He would not stop pleading. He said, "I have this date. I have a date with a woman tonight—the first date I've had in years. I know *she's the one!* If you arrest me today, she'll never go out with me!"

I thought to myself, *If he is making up this story, then he is one fabulous liar because his tears, disposition, and behavior seem incredibly real and indicative of a truthful person.* When I ran his name through the computer, he was *very* suspended all right. He had been arrested on two different occasions for driving while suspended and he had many points on his license dating back several years. Apparently, he was suspended because of his poor driving. In this case, however, I hadn't stopped him for a driving violation, merely having a taillight out.

I walked back to the car. His voice cracked as he spoke. "This-this w-woman, is my s-soul mate. I-I know she is . . ." he sniffled. "I-I've b-been looking for her for l-lifetimes! I-I know you don't believe me, but if you arrest me, w-we w-will n-never marry l-like we're s-supposed to. If you arrest me, I-I'm *sooo* s-screwed! I-I've been so lonely, and finally I f-found her." I could see he was crying, plus I believed him.

In my department patrolmen have discretion and are empowered to make decisions—whether to write a citation, for example, and ask the person to appear in court later, or to physically lodge a person in jail. What made my job difficult sometimes was that as a female officer I was often harshly judged by my male peers and accused of being too soft.

This man's arrest would have looked great on my statistics, but I felt it would clearly screw up the man's life unnecessarily. He was respectful and honest with me, so I chose to let him go. I listened to my heart. I wrote him a citation for driving while suspended and told him to walk across the street to the gas station and call a taxi. I warned him he was not allowed to drive and then I left.

I am sure he probably drove off in his car after I left, but I didn't care. He hadn't committed any traffic violation and I knew he would show up in court. It was going to cost him several hundred dollars in fines to take care of the matter and he'd probably lose another year of driving privileges. I thought nothing more about the matter and by the next day I had completely forgotten the incident.

Two years later I was still a patrolman, and I was feeling down and out because I'd been passed by several times for promotion, most likely because I was a softy. When I stopped people on patrol, I tried to be fair. When I was dispatched to crime scenes, even the most non-serious in nature, I treated people with care and dignity the way I would want to be treated. In many cases I could have said, "I'm sorry, I can't help you. This is not a police matter," or "I'm sorry, this is a civil matter, you'll have to go to small claims court," or "There were no laws broken and I have ten other calls I must go to today"—but I didn't. I helped everyone I could, even if it really wasn't my job. I was beginning to believe my department penalized me for this behavior, for being a true public servant, so I was disgruntled.

One night, I stopped yet another vehicle with a taillight out. This time, however, when the driver jumped out of his car I could tell he was angry and ready for combat. Plus he smelled strongly of intoxicants. He was obviously drunk with bloodshot eyes and slurred speech. He could barely stand up. I knew instantly I was about to get into a fight.

I said, "Sir, please get back in your car." It appeared like he wanted to run.

I said, "Okay, sir. You are now under arrest." And the fight was on!

Because it wasn't dark yet, I did not have a partner. I was on single-man patrol. As I tried to put handcuffs on the man, I was asking for backup on my radio prep. Central Dispatch could hear the man screaming in the background. He was calling me every dirty name in the book. Although I was in the best shape I had ever been, I was only five feet, two inches tall and weighed 128 pounds. This man was big. He had to be five ten and at least 250 pounds. I thought, *I'm totally screwed!* I didn't think I had a chance of avoiding injury.

He was resisting my putting the cuffs on him; soon we were tumbling in the snow bank. As we wrestled I thought maybe the snow and cold weather would affect his agility, but he just seemed to get stronger and stronger! He took several swings towards my face, which I managed to avoid. I was now eating quite a bit of snow and my hands were numb. It definitely seemed like I was going to get the worst of it.

As I continued rolling and doing somersaults in the snow with this man, I noticed the headlights of a semi-truck pull in and park behind my patrol car. The truck driver, who was fortunately a good-sized man himself, ran to my rescue. It was a bit humbling to me, but I was grateful he came to my aid.

He towered over the drunk, lifted him by his collar, and said, "This little lady said you're under arrest. You're under arrest!"

The truck driver tossed the drunk in the backseat of the patrol car. Somehow during the havoc I had managed to cuff the guy. I slammed the patrol car door and said, "If you break *anything* in my patrol car, I'll submit for a warrant for destroying police property. *That's a five-year felony!*" I was peeved.

As I shook the snow off my pants, I sheepishly looked at the truck driver and said, "Thank you. That was very nice of you to stop and help me. I am truly grateful."

He looked at me and said, "We got married!" I looked at him blankly. "You don't recognize me, do you?" He grinned.

I surveyed his face and said, "No, I'm afraid not, though you do look a little familiar." I always say this to people when they recognize me but I don't recognize them. It softens the blow to the other person, but I had absolutely no idea who this man was or where I might have seen him before.

He said, "I am the man you stopped two years ago, my car had a taillight out."

I wondered, *Does this man realize how many cars I've stopped in the course of two years? Geez!* I politely said, "Gosh, I can't remember who you are. I'm sorry."

"You stopped me on M-72, remember? I had a suspended license, and when I told you I had a date with my soul mate, you decided not to take me to jail."

Then I remembered. "Why, of course," I said, "you're the man who was so upset about losing his lady friend. Yes, I remember!"

The truck driver said, "I recognized you instantly, even though I couldn't see your face, rolling in the snow bank . . . I knew it was my turn to help you now!"

I hoped he didn't see my face turn red. Like most people, he recognized me from behind . . . I have an unusual pear-shaped body. I tried to hide my embarrassment with another "Thank you."

Then he added, "And I want you to know, I got my license back, went to truck driving school, and we did end up getting married! You made a real difference in my life."

Now my heart melted. That moment I started to feel better about the work I do.

The man said, "I believe in karma . . . I believe it was all supposed to happen this way."

I thought, *He has a lot of wisdom. What goes around, comes around—what a strange—but fortunate—series of coincidences!* Although, maybe it really was karma.

A Trooper's Debt on Christmas Day

Brian sat in his patrol car on December 25, 2005. He was parked on a wide turnout on I-395, where he could watch the cars heading north out of Spokane. He was looking for DUIs and speeders, aiming his Falcon at cars that looked like they were "over." It was almost noon and there was a lull in traffic.

He put the handheld radar on the seat beside him and turned up the FM radio. Christmas music was playing and Brian tried to count the number of Christmases he had worked as a trooper. He thought it was nineteen, counting the one he was working.

When he was a young trooper, he worked the first Christmases because he needed the money. The later ones he worked so the younger men could be with their families. Ten service stripes on his shirtsleeve and the lines on his face marked the thirty years he had spent working the road.

For some reason, Brian remembered back to the big argument that went on in his family for years. It started when Brian was four or five years old. His mother was a devout Baptist and she figured that since Brian was her only son, he most certainly was going to be a Baptist minister. His dad, on the other hand, was a logger who worked in the mountains between Colville and the Canadian border. He owned five logging trucks, two skidders, a big yarder, and had seven fulltime employees. More than anything, he wanted his son to become a doctor—not a pastor— and for sure not a logger.

Dinnertime is when the battles took place. Young Brian would take a bite of meatloaf or pot roast and scrunch down in his chair as the shelling began. "My son will become a Baptist pastor and we will send him off to Bible College! When he graduates, he can

149

come right back here to Colville Valley and pastor a nice church, close to his mother!"

The big logger's face would get red and he would struggle to keep from saying something he might regret while he slept on the couch. "Woman, it will be a cold day in a hot place before that happens! That boy has the makings of a surgeon and I have not roasted and frozen in the woods most of my life to see my son live like a pauper. Doctors make good money and they get respect—not like a gyppo logger. When he is practicing medicine he can give lots of money to a church, but this boy is going to be a doctor!" The arguments took place at least once a week.

When Brian was eleven, his dad gave him a ring that was one-of-a-kind. The jeweler in Colville that crafted it told Brian's dad that there was not another ring like it in the state. It had a wide gold band and in a strong setting in the center of was a large tiger eye stone. The jeweler placed the ring in a small box and as he wrapped it, he gave a few last words of advice to the logger. "I made the band man-sized, so he can grow into it. I will resize it for free if it's too big by the time Brian is eighteen. The tiger eye stone is supposed to bring courage, energy, and luck. It was worn by Roman soldiers for protection in battle."

Brian's dad waited until his wife was at the grocery store before handed the gift to his son. "This is what a doctor wears, son. Keep it hidden until your ring finger is big enough to wear it. And don't tell your mother about this ring, even if she buys you a wooden pulpit to practice preaching on."

The summer of 1974 was hot, with lots of forest fires. In the early fall, the fire danger in the Colville National Forest was so bad that all logging was shut down for a couple of weeks. So, Brian's dad declared a holiday and the family left for Spokane on a warm Saturday morning.

His parents were playing nice with each other; talking and chuckling as they passed by Deer Park and sailed on towards

Spokane. The trooper that pulled in behind them paced his dad at twenty over and turned on his light bar and rolled the big logger over to the side. The trooper walked up to the driver's side of the car and wrote his dad a ticket for less than he could have.

Brian watched every move the state trooper made and noted every detail of his uniform, hat, badge, and gun. He listened to the words the lawman said and how he conducted himself without arrogance, but with dignity. It was as if a hidden door opened for Brian—he knew beyond any doubt he had found his calling.

The next seven years flew for Brian. By his senior year, the ring fit perfectly and he wore it with pride, picturing a Roman soldier, strong and brave, or a Washington State Trooper. The battles for his future became wars; but even though his mom and dad were both stubborn, he was their son—and he had a double dose of resolve. He only grinned when they badgered him about his plans.

In late August, the letter Brian had hoped for came in the mail. His mother, with the look of a general who had lost a war, handed her son the envelope from the Washington State Patrol in Olympia. His dad's scowl grew as Brian opened the letter and grinned from ear to ear. Brian had been accepted as a cadet and his class would start in January. There were several months of wailing and gnashing of teeth by his parents—but Brian became a trooper.

For thirty years he lived the life and wore the badge. Along the way, he lost his dad and his marriage. He had a daughter in Spokane whose husband was in Iraq.

His daughter and son-in-law had a daughter named Ellie, who was eight years old and was the light of Brian's life. He adored the child, and she loved him back. She named Brian Paw Paw before she could walk.

Brian broke out of his reverie and checked a passing car with his Falcon. He thought again about his folks and the turns in the road that life took. Sometimes, lately, he wondered if becoming a pastor or doctor wouldn't have been a better way. A trooper's life wasn't for everyone, though he had found himself, found his reason in it.

He had stopped speeders and drunks and been to a thousand wrecks, where without his help some people would have died. Many times he got blood on his uniform, trying to keep a victim from bleeding out or giving up. He remembered the one he called the "Christmas Wreck."

Brian had been twenty-one, with only two years on the job. A family was headed north on Highway 2, towards Newport, when the father lost control of the car on black ice and slid into an oncoming milk truck.

Brian was the first on the scene. The trucker's injuries were minor since he sat above the car. The father was unconscious with a concussion and several fractures. Brian saw the passenger, a woman, who was in bad shape. At least one arm was broken and she was covered in blood. She had been cut by a shard of glass across her upper chest and her brachial artery was spurting blood. Brian went around to her side and, with hands as strong as the logger who sired him, put direct pressure on the gouging wound.

Far away, he heard the ambulance siren. When he saw the blood the woman had lost, he felt helpless and alone. What happened next made the hair on the back of his neck stand up.

A small boy, maybe six, had been behind the passenger seat, afraid to come out after the wreck. He was bruised, but had his seat belt on and was in one piece. The boy leaned over the seat and studied the trooper and his mother and father. Then, with words the young trooper would never forget, the boy prayed. "I call to you in heaven, and I know that you can hear me. I do not ask for myself, because I know that you will take care of me. I ask for my dad and my mother, that you help her to live. They need each other. Thank you." The little boy watched the big trooper, who was covered with his mother's blood, as his strong hand kept pressure on the wound. Eventually an ambulance arrived to take the victims to the hospital.

A call from Kim, the dispatcher, broke Brian's reverie. She asked Brian to call her back on his cell phone. He always laughed and joked with Kim, even in the most stressful situations, as a way to maintain sanity. Kim wasn't laughing or joking now. She was quiet and reserved. There was a long pause before she spoke. "Ummm, Brian, I have some bad news. Your daughter and granddaughter were involved in an accident about a half-hour ago. A drunk T-boned their car on the passenger side. Your daughter is in stable condition, but, umm, your granddaughter has a punctured lung, several fractures, and internal bleeding. They don't expect her to make it."

Brian was shaking as he ended the cell call. He told dispatch he was enroute to Deaconess Hospital. He noticed, as he drove down Division Street, that there were Christmas lights that he had never seen before. And he couldn't remember Gonzaga University being lit up like it was. He was in a slow-motion grieving stage.

The best thing in the trooper's life would soon be gone. Ellie was the sun that rose and set in his life. He parked his patrol car in the hospital parking lot and walked up to ER. He found a nurse he had known for years and asked her to tell him the truth about Ellie. "Brian, she is in bad shape. The prognosis is not good. She will be operated on in the next hour. The doctor on duty is young, but he is good. I'll come find you when there is a change."

Brian walked numbly, putting one foot in front of the other, to the empty waiting room. The grieving trooper stood six-feet-two. He was a mass of muscle and bone. He was a master marksman, and had never lost a fight—but as he sat in the deep cushioned chair he felt helpless. He covered his face in his hands as the worst nightmare of his life played on.

The place was empty as tears made his big hands glisten. After a few minutes, two voices came into the room, just two men passing through on their way to a family gathering. They lowered their voices when they saw the grieving trooper and were almost out the other door when one of the men stopped in mid-sentence. "It's him! It's the trooper with the ring!"

Five minutes later, one of the men sat next to Brian while his brother, Dr. Ashley, scrubbed for surgery to operate on Ellie. Dr. Ashley was known by his peers as one of the finest surgeons in the state of Washington.

For the second time in his life, Brian heard the voice, much older now, as a prayer was sent for help from above. "I call to you in heaven, because I know that you hear me. It is probably not fair that I call on you to pay my debt, but this is not the first time. This is the trooper who saved my mother from bleeding to death. My brother, the surgeon, would not have been born a year later if it were not for this man. I am asking not for myself, but for this man, that you keep his granddaughter in this world. He needs her. So, I ask you to pay my Christmas debt. Thank you".

Pastor Ashley, who pastored the largest Baptist church in Spokane, sat beside the trooper, while three doors down his brother operated on the young girl. The surgeon labored, but so did his brother and also the angels, strong and kind, who came not to take her with them, but to bring her back.

Brian did not work on December 25, 2006. It turned out he needed most of the day as it took him six hours to assemble the playhouse he bought for Ellie and two hours for them to enjoy tea and cookies.

Tom Brosman,
Senior Telecommunications Specialist
Washington State Patrol

Frog Time

I am a police polygraphist. A young girl with the weight of the world on her shoulders walked into my examination room one morning. She was pretty, but shy and introverted—at first, she didn't want to look at me. One of my initial thoughts when I shook her hand, was how sensitive yet powerful she was. And although little had been said—I already *knew*, somehow, she was truthful. As with everyone who enters my office, I gave her the benefit of the doubt and remained neutral. I could tell it would take time to gain her trust.

As we reviewed why she was here and talked briefly about her home life, thoughts of my grandfather, a man of Gaelic tradition, went through my mind. My grandfather loved frogs. He said frogs had a beauty and magic behind their appearance. I remembered saying to my grandfather, "Oh, you mean like in fairy tales, when a princess kisses a frog and it turns into a prince?" He laughed and said, "Why, yes! Most fairy tales have some Gaelic tradition." My grandfather was a wise man. I didn't know why I had suddenly remembered all of this.

As the polygraph examination progressed, I could tell this young girl was different. I sensed that she was *aware*. I reminded myself that my sole purpose in being here, though, was to determine her truthfulness.

I allowed her to speak about her life, to share how she felt, and to give her side of the story. She was accused of stealing deposit money from a place where she worked. The case facts and circumstances seemed so clear that the employer had temporarily suspended her. The more I listened, however, the more she opened up, and the more I realized she probably didn't commit the crime.

The strange part was when she started to talk about a pet frog she had when she was younger. She said she loved frogs, but that she accidentally killed her frog one night when she forgot about him. She explained the house had become so cold when the heat went out that the water in the frog's tank started to freeze. When she finally remembered her frog the next morning, she found him frozen to the layer of water. She cried, then laughed, and finally said, "I don't even know why I'm telling you this . . . maybe it's because I feel like that poor frog, frozen and unable to move. You're the only person who has listened to me and what I have to say. I really didn't do this crime! The facts look bad, I know; but I didn't do it!" She was teary-eyed; but sweet and sincere.

I reminded myself our frog connection had nothing to do with the *polygraph test* itself—but how freaky was this? I'd just thought earlier about my grandfather and what he said about frogs—and now she's telling me about a pet frog she loved that died. And then she sees the frog's death as a metaphor for her own position: accused of a crime and unable to prove her innocence! I thought to myself, *Without even running the charts, I don't think she did this crime. I know I'm not supposed to judge, and I'll remain neutral . . . I could be wrong . . . but there is something just too weird going on here about frogs!*

Everything about the polygraph examination went smoothly. I showed her how polygraph works, and we ran a practice test. She was relieved, but still apprehensive.

I ran three charts total. I was fairly certain she was passing the test; but as always, I score out the charts when I'm finished. I do this in the same room with the subject, while continually watching his or her behavior out of the corner of my eye. She waited patiently, but concerned, as I scored each chart. I allowed her to get up and stretch. She drank her soda, and then sat back down.

Suddenly I saw the happiest, biggest smile on her face—like she'd had a sudden revelation or something. "What? Did

I do something silly?" I asked, as I finished up with her chart evaluation. Her eyes welled up with joyful tears, as she stared underneath the table, her head half-cocked as she strained to see something better. My chair seemed to be in the line of her vision. She looked dreamy. In a soft-spoken but jubilant and confident voice she proclaimed, "I passed! I know I passed the test!"

I gently smiled and said, "How do you know?" I knew she had definitely passed, but I hadn't given her my decision yet.

She giggled and said, "There's a FROG underneath your table—in the corner, half-hidden behind that old flowerpot . . ." Her eyes gleamed with inner knowing as she looked at me.

I spun my chair around and, sure enough, underneath the table was a ceramic frog—a beautifully handcrafted frog—that I had *never* seen before! I knew instantly my wife must have put it there. She always said she'd surprise me with a frog one day, and she had visited the office a couple weeks ago.

I don't understand what to make of this synchronistic incident,

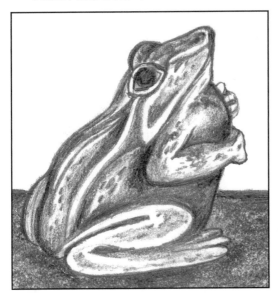

but it certainly is a wonderful and mysterious concept. The young lady passed the polygraph test with flying colors, so I didn't *need* the frog thoughts to help me—though it did make this exam a mystical and spiritual experience.

Murder 101

Bill Brady, a pillar of the community and assistant quartermaster at the VFW hall, was dead. He had been shot six times. Unfortunately, there were no leads in the case. The victim was not involved in any criminal activity nor did he associate with people of questionable character. It appeared, in fact, to be the perfect murder. Everyone loved Bill very much, including his best friend, David Goldstick, who had found him dead.

A crime-scene investigator, Sgt. Steve Hickman, told me that the bullets that killed Bill were .380s and I should be looking for a .380 in my investigation. I reviewed this information with my team and then we dispersed to conduct initial interviews. In response to a message I received from the Holy Spirit, I decided to interview David Goldstick myself.

As a police officer, I don't often talk about the messages I receive from the Holy Spirit because I don't want to be labeled by fellow officers as a *religious nut* or somebody *out in left field*, but the truth is the Holy Spirit of God gives me guidance and direction in my life. So, when the thought *Interview David* spoke to me, I selected David Goldstick as my person to interview. I met David at the scene of the crime and asked him about the events that led up to his finding the body, his association with Bill Brady, and his family and friends. As we sat in the patrol car and talked, David came across as truthful and sincere. I was not suspicious of him at all. I also asked him if he had any guns. He answered, "No, my mom doesn't allow any guns in the house."

Afterward, when I was back at the office, I learned that David *did* have a gun registered, though it was a .357 magnum not a .380 like was used in the killing. The inconsistency made me curious, so I decided to ask him to return to the scene and be re-interviewed. He agreed. As before, I talked with him in the car.

David acted confused when I confronted him with the safety registration card. He swore he didn't have a .357—had never owned one. At this point, he seemed a bit uptight, but understandably so. He had found his best friend dead; that would be traumatic for anybody.

We were parked in front of the VFW building. There had been a fire there recently and the building was under construction. A makeshift office had been established next door in a pole barn owned by Bill's daughter and son-in-law. It occurred to me that the murder might be about money. When I asked David where the VFW's financial books were kept, he said in some filing cabinets in the office next door. Maybe money was missing and that was the motive for Bill's murder.

I asked David if the filing cabinets were kept locked and he said yes. I asked who had the keys. He said there were two sets. He had one set, and the other set was Bill's. I decided to secure all the information in those file cabinets so it could be analyzed. I asked David if we could we get the keys and he said, "Yes, we can do that."

At first he said the keys were in his house and then he said they were in his car, which was at a house where he worked as a caretaker; but then he said, "No, wait . . . they're in my house." That is when I got the second major message from the Holy Spirit: *Obtain David's set of keys now.*

"What's at your house?" I asked.

"The keys . . . maybe. Well, just take me back to my car."

So we took a four-minute drive to where he was working as a caretaker, turned into the driveway, and I pulled up behind his black Jimmy. When I parked the car, David got out, and said, "Wait here."

What happened next I absolutely attribute to prompting from

God. Instead of waiting, I got out of the car. I don't know why other than I felt a strong need to get out of the car when David told me to stay. As he walked to the passenger side of the Jimmy, I walked up to the driver's side. The rear door window was rolled down about eight inches. As I walked by it, I looked into the car. The rear seat was folded down, and sticking out from underneath it was an object. It didn't immediately register what it was. After I looked at it more closely I could tell it was wood and that it had been cut. I immediately said to him, "Hey, can I look in your car?" David said I could. I opened the door and pulled out a sawed-off Rueger 10.22 rifle. The barrel had been cut off, a hose coupling had been placed on the barrel, and attached to that was a lawn mower muffler!

I've been asked how I feel when I get messages from the Holy Spirit. I can only say they just come to me. I only know that God is talking to me and that He has helped me solve many cases.

I held up the sawed-off shotgun and said, "What's this?"

He replied, "It is what I keep in my car. I take trips downstate, to Bay City and Ann Arbor, and I keep it in my car for protection." I spotted another box in the Jimmy and asked what it was. He said it was for silencing guns.

I went back to my patrol car and called for a marked unit. I wanted a warrant to search the Jimmy. My intention was to take David back to the VFW, leave him there, have the marked unit stay with the Jimmy and secure it, while I went to the Prosecutor's Office to get a search warrant. Before driving away, though, I took a short taped statement from David about the ownership of the rifle, the box and what he did with the box, and why these items were in his vehicle. I figured at some point I would need to deal with the gun being sawed off and the silencer being affixed to it. These facts were getting in the way of solving the murder since I knew we were looking for a .380, not a .22, but it was suspicious that he had the gun when he had earlier assured me he owned none. On the other hand, David was convincing about having the gun in his car for protection. He said, "I know I'm in trouble for *that*" and he nodded at the .22, "but I didn't do the other thing," which I took to mean the murder of Bill Brady.

It was a sunny day and David was wearing eyeglasses that darkened in sunlight so I couldn't see his eyes clearly, though it looked to me like there were tears forming in his eyes. I thought, *Are his eyes tearing up? Are they actually?* It seemed like they were, so as sympathetically as I could I said, "You know, Dave, a good man like you must have really had your back up against a wall to have done something like this . . ." He nodded his head affirmatively. As soon as he did that, I "mirandized" him. Technically, I didn't have to read him his rights, because I hadn't arrested him, but I obeyed the urge. I'm glad I did. I turned on the tape recorder and took another taped statement from David. He admitted shooting Bill Brady. He took me to the murder weapon and the silencer box that was used and showed me the ammunition he had hidden in another vehicle in the garage at the house where he was a caretaker. The victim's blood was there, too.

Later, when we inspected the filing cabinet, I learned that David had embezzled a significant amount of money from the VFW and that Bill had figured it out and was going to turn David in.

Later, David's attorney said that my being so adamant about getting the keys to the file cabinet and finding the .22 and silencer were probably the turning points in our case and led to his client's confession. I have to believe he was correct. There were .380 casings inside the silencer box I had seen and David probably figured they would link him to the case.

Whether you call it intuition or being led by the Holy Spirit, unexplained urges led me to solve this crime. It wasn't great police work. I just listened.

The Flying Snowmobile

Houghton Lake is a large, beautiful inland body of water in central Michigan that freezes over in the winter and enables snowmobilers to "shanty hop" all over it. The wide-open space allows them to accelerate at high rates of speed.

In January of each year, I brace myself for Tip-Up Town, U.S.A., an annual ice-fishing festival that attracts hundreds of snowmobilers to Houghton Lake.

One late afternoon, I was dispatched to a lakeside residence. It was a seasonal home that the year-round neighbors were watching over. The homeowners were not due back until spring. The house sets back about one hundred feet from the shoreline on a slight hill, with a large oak tree between the house and the lake. The tree is about forty feet from the water and adjacent to the house.

When I arrived, the neighbors were scratching their heads. A snowmobile that was still running, was bucked up against the oak tree. None of the neighbors had approached the idling snowmobile. There were no footwear impressions in the snow leading up to the snowmobile or walking away from it. I thought this was weird. There was some damage to the front end of the sled, but no apparent damage to the tree.

My partner and I began to look for the driver. We imagined all the possibilities. Footwear impressions should have been evident—yet there were none. Thinking the worst, we walked down to the lake. Maybe the driver had hit thin ice and fallen through. I noticed an obvious snowmobile track that stopped just at the shoreline where there is a slight rise on the terrain, like a small snow bank; but nothing indicated the driver fell through the ice. We walked a huge circumference around the lake and the house, thinking the driver must have been thrown from the vehicle.

I walked back to the shoreline, looked at the tree, and then at the house in the background. I thought the snowmobile could have gone airborne after hitting the rise in the shoreline, especially if it was running at a high rate of speed. Then I saw damage on the tree trunk about ten feet up.

Suddenly I felt a small breeze brush across my face and happened to look up again at the house. The vertical blinds in the window appeared to move and I saw movement inside the house. It was strange that the blinds moved with the wind. There wasn't supposed to be anyone home.

I walked up towards the house and saw a window was completely busted out. I moved a few blinds with one finger and peered in. Shattered glass was everywhere, but more noticeable was a man! He was dressed in snowmobile garb, lying half-unconscious underneath the dining room table!

I quickly climbed through the window to check his condition. He groaned and moved as I made my way to him. I asked, "Are you okay? What's your name?" He had an injury to his head, there was blood dripping down his face and his helmet was noticeably cracked. I gently shined my light near his eyes to check his pupils. When he groaned again I smelled intoxicants on his breath.

I immediately called Central Dispatch to send an ambulance. Then I asked the man, "Do you even know what day it is?" I also urged him to stay still.

"Memorial Day," he groaned, rather indignantly.

Our accident re-constructionist said this was one of the strangest, most miraculous incidents he'd ever worked on. The snowmobile was, indeed, travelling at a high rate of speed. It went airborne at the rise in the shoreline, hit the tree, and then landed at its final resting place at the base of the tree. The driver separated from the snowmobile, probably at the rise of the bank, flying approximately one hundred feet through the front window of the house, blowing all the glass inside, and finally landing underneath the kitchen table.

Apparently, the driver entered through the window horizontally and parallel to the ground. His head hit one window edge while his feet hit the other edge, fracturing his skull and crushing both limbs. The blood, his condition, and damage to the house showed this. It was amazing he didn't hit the eaves and get his body slicked in two or hit a smaller front window that was in his line of travel. He was lucky to have survived.

Skunked

Patrol desk, Anderson," I said after I punched line three. "How can I help you?" It had been a busy evening. The phone was ringing off the wall. I was alone at the desk—with the exception of the desk sergeant, who was sitting behind me reading the newspaper. For some unknown reason he felt above picking up the phone and answering it. All six of the lines were lit up.

Earlier in the day, a fourteen-year-old kid had raped and murdered an eighty-five-year old lady on the city's west side. They picked him up southwest of Lansing but not before he killed a policeman. The cop had pulled him over and the kid just shot him in the face. Dead. A fourteen-year-old kid. A cop killer. It's hard to figure.

"Just where in the hell have you been? That phone rang more than twenty times. Is that why I pay taxes?" came a male voice from the other end of the line.

I listened to the man vent his frustrations. "What can I do for you, sir?" I asked when he finally took a breath.

"Well, you can start by giving me your name. Someone's going to hear about this! This is bullshit. The money I pay for taxes and I can't get you bastards to even answer the phone!" He wanted me to apologize but that would never happen. Never apologize to a fool. He continued to ramble on and on.

"Hey, Anderson," came the dispatcher's voice over the desk monitor. "There's a lady on line six with a problem you can take care of. I told her we didn't have any cars to send her. See if you can handle it over the phone for me, will ya?"

I flipped the button on the console and said, "Yeah, sure. You might tell her there are five lines ahead of her." The dispatcher didn't respond.

"The name is Anderson, Richard Anderson. Badge #324," I said. "Now, how can I help you?" There was silence. "Hello, you still there?" I asked. I still had five lines flashing.

"I want to talk with your supervisor," he bellowed.

"Sure, no problem." I put him on hold.

"Sergeant, line three is for you!" I went to line four.

"Patrol desk, Anderson," I said. "How can I help you?"

"Who's on line three? What do they want?" asked the sergeant, looking over the top of his newspaper. I ignored him. Several minutes passed, much advice was exchanged before I finally got to line six.

"Patrol desk, Anderson," I said. "How can I help you?" The lady on the other end sounded old. Her voice was shaky.

"Well, officer, I have a problem. It was such a nice day that I decided to open up the house and air it out. I opened all the windows and both the front and back doors. I saw it scamper across the back foyer, where the kids used to keep their boots when they were younger. Now they are all grown up . . ." There was a long pause. "I wish Harold was here; he would know what to do. I just don't know what to do," she added.

"Well, where is Harold? When will he be back?" I asked.

"Oh, he's been dead for fifteen years now."

All the lines were lit up again. "Anderson, who's on line three?" demanded the sergeant. "It's not my 'ol lady, is it?" I cupped my hand over the phone and turned around to look at him.

"It's some asshole who wants to complain about the way I'm answering the phone, Sarge." The sergeant was well into the sports section of the paper.

"Well, I don't want to talk to him. Tell him something. Tell him to call back in an hour. Tell him anything."

I turned back around and returned to the old lady on line six.

She was still rambling. "He took sick in the shop, Harold did, and he wouldn't leave to come home. Said he only had about two hours left. That was the way he was," she reminisced.

"Ma'am. Ma'am." I interrupted. "Listen, I need to find out what your problem is. Why did you call the police?"

"Oh, it's that thing in the basement. That thing that scampered down the steps," she advised.

"Well, what is it? Is it a squirrel?" I asked. "Just go down there with a broom and chase it back up the steps. It will run outside just as fast as it ran inside." I hung up the phone and pressed another line.

"Patrol desk, Anderson," I said.

"My husband just beat me up! Send me the cops!"

"Anderson, did you take care of line three yet?" asked the sergeant.

"Hell, no! He wants to talk with you!" I responded.

"Patrol desk, Anderson," I said into line five. "How can I help you?" It was the old lady again. She had moved from line six to line five.

"I wish to speak with Officer Anderson again, please." She remembered my name.

"This is Officer Anderson," I said.

"Sir," she began. "I'm afraid your idea is not going to work. I do wish my Harold was here. He would know just what to do. He was such a great man," she added.

"Ma'am, we just don't have a car to send over to take care of a squirrel in your basement. There are simply too many pressing emergencies going on right now," I advised. "I'm sorry, but that is just the way it is."

"Officer, officer," she interrupted. "This is not a squirrel. It's a skunk!" Shit. A damn skunk!

"Anderson!" demanded the sergeant. "Did you take care of line three yet? It's still blinking!"

"No, sir, I sure didn't. I haven't had a chance," I answered.

"Well, take care of that asshole," he demanded. "I'm not going to talk to him."

"A skunk, huh?" I questioned. "Are you sure it's a skunk and not a cat?"

"Well, officer, I certainly know the difference between a skunk and a cat," she reprimanded. "If only Harold ..."

"Yeah, yeah, I know. Harold would know just what to do, but he's not here," I said. "How about taking a can of something, like cat food or sardines, and make a trail from the basement up the steps and outside the house? Maybe the skunk will eat his way up the steps and outside. Then, just close the door behind him when he goes out." There was a pause on the other end of the line. All of the other lines were flashing.

"If only Harold were here, he would know what to do ..." repeated the old weak voice.

I took a chance on line three again. "Patrol desk, Anderson," I said. "How can I help you?" The same gruff voice was on the other end. He had been on hold for over ten minutes now.

"I don't want to talk to you. I want to talk to your supervisor! I told you that an hour ago!" I put him back on hold and advised the sergeant of the call. This time the sergeant ignored me.

The hectic pace continued for two hours or more. One call right after the other. It was crazy. There must have been a full moon out that night. I punched line three again. "Patrol desk, how can I help you?" I asked.

"I wish to speak to Officer Anderson," said the old lady.

"This is Anderson," I said. There was another long pause.

"Your idea didn't work, Officer Anderson. I did just what you said and now there are two skunks in my basement." Two skunks. Shit! Now what? I was starting to wish Harold had been there because maybe he would have known what to do.

"Can you hold the line for a minute?" I requested and then put her back on hold.

"Hey, Sarge, you're a hunter, aren't you?" I asked.

"Sure, never miss a chance," he answered.

"Well, I was just getting ready to go grab a sandwich with Gillis. Can you take care of the lady on line three for me? It has to do with wild game." He agreed. I grabbed my hat and headed for the elevator.

"Yes, Officer Anderson is a fine lad," came the sergeant's voice from behind his desk. "Harold? Well, where is he? When will he be back? Oh, I'm so sorry." I had just reached the elevator door when I heard him say, "Sardines?" Then he yelled, "Two skunks?! Did you say two skunks?! Hey, Anderson!! Come back here!!" The elevator doors closed. It started down. I was on my way to lunch. I smiled.

Gillis was parked out back waiting for me. We checked out of service with dispatch and went to a coney island restaurant for a sandwich. "Would one of you be Officer Anderson?" asked the young waitress. "There is a phone call for you in the kitchen." I followed her through the swinging doors and picked up the phone. It was dispatch. They wanted Gillis and me to drive to a sheriff's department one hour away to pick up the fourteen-year-old cop killer. We were to take him directly to the juvenile facilities where they would be expecting us.

I'll always remember the lad's face. You would have never guessed he was that young. He looked like a hardened twenty-year-old. He reminded me of a caged animal. He was sitting in a cell on a bench with a straitjacket on.

"What's the deal with the jacket?" questioned Gillis.

"We can't keep him in handcuffs. If you put them on, he'll hand them to you in about thirty seconds," said the desk sergeant. "I don't know how he does it but he does."

We kept him in the straitjacket and delivered him to the juvenile facility. The lady on duty at the detention home opened the door for us and was shocked when she saw the boy was strapped into a straitjacket. She ordered us to remove it at once. I reminded her who this kid was and that he had killed two people. My response fell on deaf ears. She assured Gillis and me that our supervisor would be hearing about this matter.

Gillis and I returned to the station. We were already two hours past our normal quitting time. The third-shift sergeant flagged us down. Sure enough, the lady was true to her word. "I've got an abuse complaint on you two. I'll need a report before you go home." We both sat down at a computer and wrote out a lengthy report. We explained our actions and the reasons we did what we did, always keeping in mind the possibility of a lawsuit.

When I was almost finished with the report, the desk officer yelled, "Hey, Anderson! Do you know what that Malone kid looks like or what he was wearing when you left him?" Gillis looked at me. I looked at Gillis.

"She let that little !&*&#@** get away, didn't she?" Gillis groaned.

The desk officer held his hand over the receiver of the phone and added, "He slipped away from the juvenile home just now. All Mary Poppins has to say is 'The little skunk just slipped away. Geez, I don't know where he could have gone.'"

Gillis and I turned in our reports and headed home. It was now three o'clock in the morning. I wondered if the public had any idea what could happen in a cop's day at work.

My wife and I have a private joke. She uses it when she thinks I've had a bad day. She will ask me, "Well, what was the score last night?" and I usually come back with, "Well, we got shut out. One to nothing or two to nothing or whatever." We usually lost; but once in awhile we'd get lucky and score.

That morning was a different. When a cop gets killed, it takes the life right out of you. I hadn't even processed all that had happened. I poured milk on my oatmeal and just quietly replied, "We got skunked."

A River Wide and Deep

by Tom Brosman

In shirts of blue, in the dark of night
They roll to wrecks and danger
Before the medics come on scene
They comfort injured strangers.

Troopers are idols of kids who dream
One day they'll drive a patrol car
Behind a wheel, so white it gleams
But it's not the way things really are.

Things you would never want to see—
First at crash, the awful scene
Broken glass, blood—fatalities
Uniform far from clean.

A trooper with a few years on, sees
The best and the worst in people.
The number of friends the trooper trusts
Dwindles down to digits single.

Oh, lots of people do brag and say
They are going to be a trooper
But when the chance is on the table,
They choose to be a plumber.

Only a few, a vital few,
Wear the badge proudly and live the life
Work the nights and weekends, too
And don't complain the cost is high.

There are those that talk and those that do
A river deep between the two.
Lots of troopers pay the price
And proudly wear the shirt of blue.

*"Let not the conceit of intellect hinder thee
from worshipping mystery."*

M.F. Tupper, *Proverbial Philosophy*

Unexplainable
Phenomena

This culmination of unexplainable phenomena addresses the "higher end" of the transpersonal perspective and may help to expand our grasp of what may be possible in the Universe. Such encounters address the range of our potential for interaction and, thus, go beyond the person. It includes encounters with alien beings, UFOs, shape-shifters, curving bullets, and other anomalous phenomena such as out-of-body experiences. The nature of this chapter is not to prove or argue with these exceptional police experiences but to simply keep an open mind and listen with deference.

"These experiences . . . seem to catalyze a process that eventually can lead to the realization of the person's higher human potential. Lives, worldviews, and even identities can be transformed. When this process of transformation is initiated, an exceptional experience becomes an exceptional human experience."

Rhea A. White, "Becoming more Human as We Work,"
Transpersonal Methods for the Social Sciences

"It happens, by a common vice of human nature, that we trust most to, and are most seriously frightened at, things which are strange and unknown."

Caesar, *De Bello Civili*

Bizarre Weather

When I was a brand-new recruit at the St. Joseph Post I was assigned to work with Larry Boger. Trooper Boger was a short, stocky, stubborn, old man with a gruff voice, deep lines on his face, gray hair, and a cigarette in his mouth. He was the epitome of what we call "old school." I was green and shy.

We were having coffee at the local gas station when dispatch requested assistance on a train/pedestrian accident. This type of accident is usually fatal, so my heart started to pound. I had never been to a serious accident before.

We arrived at the train tracks in the area where a pedestrian was supposed to have been hit by the train. We didn't see anything immediately. It was a sunny winter day and the sky was blue.

Larry advised, "Take your time and walk carefully down the tracks." (Larry always sauntered to my fast pace.)

As he grabbed the radio prep from the patrol car, I got out. These were the days when you had to have a "repeater" in the patrol car for the hand-held radio to work, and sometimes reception was poor.

Larry was not overly excited, so I tried to copy his behavior. They always said in recruit school that new troopers are reflections of their senior officers. I wanted to act cool, stay relaxed, and be just like him.

Larry suddenly stopped. I thought to myself, *Oh my God*, but Larry remained calm. Larry put his cigarette in his mouth, took a puff, and slowly blew out the smoke.

Then he matter-of-factly said into the prep, "Central dispatch, we got a leg." My heart was racing but I pretended to be calm. We continued walking down the track.

Larry stopped, put his cigarette in his mouth and took another puff. He looked up into the sky, and this time he blew smoke rings. He said into the prep, "Central, we got us an arm." His voice was monotone, and he seemed undaunted. We continued walking.

Larry came to an abrupt stop. He had spotted something in the snow bank. He took another puff of his cigarette and said, "Central, we got us a torso now."

The snow was so bright I had to adjust my eyes. I was trying hard to see what he was looking at. In shock, I said, "Oh, okay. Now I can see him!" I thought, *Wow, how does Larry stay so calm? I don't know if I can ever be like him.*

Larry looked at me and like a teacher, said, "Now young man, walk over there and see if he's alive. Check and see if you can get a pulse." I was so sheepish! The torso lay motionless, its head partially facedown in the snow bank. It was probably one hundred feet from the train track. I thought, *Holy mackerel, that poor guy had to be hit pretty hard to be laying way over here.*

As I approached the torso, I could feel myself hyperventilating. I was scared. I had never seen a dead body in this condition before. My pulse throbbed in my neck. Very slowly and cautiously I extended two fingers towards his neck to check for a pulse.

Suddenly, the man swung his body around, his face only inches from my nose, and blurted out, "Hey, I think I need an ambulance!"

The man's eyeballs were nearly popped out of the sockets, like a freak at a Halloween party. I could almost touch the whites of his eyes! I let out a shriek, jumped back nearly ten feet, and landed flat on my ass in the snow! Yes, it was a sight Larry and I never forgot.

The train had pushed and dragged the man at such a high rate of speed that his limbs were cut and thrown from the track in different directions. The man's limbs were severed so quickly and it was so cold outside that his blood coagulated and the man survived.

Two months later, I stopped him on the roadway for speeding. He proceeded to show me his prostheses! He was delighted to see me and enthusiastically said, "Thank you *so much* for helping me! *See?* I got a new arm and a new leg and I can drive!"

I decided not to give him a ticket. Somehow it just didn't seem appropriate.

Colors Never Seen Before

When I read the local newspaper headline "Mysterious Flying Object Might Have Been a Planet," I shook my head in frustration. I couldn't believe it. The unidentified flying object (UFO) I saw hovering over this lady's pole barn was *not* a planet rising over the horizon! I wanted to shake some sense into the local college astronomer who suggested it. Even NASA engineers said the object was not a planet and gave their opinion that the metal was not manmade. I still have their report. And, fortunately, I videotaped the event . . .

It happened one early morning just before Christmas. It was still dark outside. My desk sergeant received a call from an excited, but frazzled, thirty-some-year-old lady who reported a "thing" hovering over her pole barn. She wanted to know what it was. I was dispatched around 6:30.

Both the sergeant and I admit we thought the call was from a "mental," given the fact so many people had recently been released from a state mental hospital in our area. To this day, however, I regret not arriving at this woman's house sooner, when the UFO was closest to the ground.

After I took my time writing a citation for a typical speeder on his way to work, I arrived on her front porch, and knocked on the door. I wasn't too excited about this visit.

The woman answered and appeared visibly shaken. "Did you see it? Did you see it? Did you see it when you pulled into the driveway?"

I said, "Nope. 'Fraid not." I was unenthusiastic.

It should be noted that I am a fifty-year-old, cantankerous police canine handler, and have been a trooper for many years. I am conservative, a member of the school board, and a Christian Protestant. I may not attend church regularly, and I smoke cigarettes like a fiend, but I'm a quiet-spoken, mild-mannered guy who loves his family very much.

The woman urgently beckoned me in. "Then come in! Come with me! Right now! I will show you." She grabs me by the hand and hustles me through the kitchen and dining room to her back sliding doors. I stepped out on the deck and suddenly *my knees buckled!* I looked up and was *shocked!* I felt all the blood drain from my face. My eyes must have been big as tennis balls. Even my body started to quiver, which is very unlike me. I had seen some strange things in my police career, but *nothing* like this.

This UFO was *massive!* It was as big as half a football field and hovered silently above this woman's pole barn. Apparently it had risen since she'd first spotted it—but I could still see it clearly. The colors were amazing. I was scared and excited.

The lady was grateful I had come as she requested. Later that day, even Paul Harvey said it was the wisest thing the woman could have done—to call the state police. I don't know if I would have believed just one person's story. As we found later, it became important that we had each other to talk to.

I radioed my sergeant and advised him that this sighting was no prank and that the woman had a legitimate concern. My voice rarely cracks over the radio, but it did that day.

I know, you might think I'm a trooper gone wacky, but the object we saw could not have been from this world. It was too weird. I'll never forget how silent it was.

It looked like the old-fashioned flying saucer in the *Lost in Space* television show, but the metal and its composition was different. As we gazed up, we saw the bottom of it. It was a strange, ethereal, brilliant array of colors and lights, interweaving and dancing over and under each other—difficult to describe well. The bottom looked open and hollow. These brilliant colors and shapes resembled Honeycomb cereal, all woven together. That's the only way I can describe it. We commented to each other how the colors did not look real. They were colors we had never seen before—and they were BEAUTIFUL! I learned later that scientists believe there are other colors in the universe that we haven't seen with our eyes. I think we were true witnesses to this concept.

Still shot from the videotape provided by the officer.

The lady had called her neighbor, Michael, just before I arrived. When Michael looked out his kitchen window, as she requested, all he could see was lightning bolts, radiating above her barn. He had to put his robe on and walk over to get a look at it.

I find it weird that neither Michael nor I could see the object at certain angles. It was only until Michael came over that he saw it, too. There was little obstruction in our initial views, from the driveway or from Michael's kitchen window, yet neither of us could see it from those vantage points. (Maybe this is what they mean by "cloaking" in science fiction.)

At first the lady and I were going to try and assemble a new video camera that was wrapped underneath her Christmas tree, but then we decided we might not figure it out in time to videotape the UFO. So, Michael ran next door and retrieved an old video camera he had stored away. Michael videotaped some wonderful clips of the object, though it seemed to get higher and higher in the sky as time went on.

The UFO was visible for almost two hours, from 6:30 A.M. to 8:30 A.M. I can hardly explain how it disappeared from view. It was moving, but it wasn't. It just didn't seem real, yet it was clear as day to the naked eye and to the video camera.

The UFO was completely silent the whole time, yet the lady's three dogs knew it was there! Perhaps it made a sound that humans could not hear but dogs could, or perhaps the lights affected them—whatever it was, they were petrified! Two of her dogs hid in the doghouse and would not come out when she called. A third dog, an Akita, hid under a bed in the house. Akitas are rarely afraid of anything.

When we first observed it, the morning was still dark, so there was some fog and haze around it, which caused the colors to shift and gleam and look quite eerie in the night sky. Plus, it was so big! As it rose above the barn and the sky got lighter, you could see the metal and the composition better. It had an outer shell that seemed to be spinning.

After about an hour, three military jets flew over the top of the house, as if to inspect it. As the jets flew over, the lights went out on the UFO, and then they came back on once the jets were gone. I called my sergeant and asked him to check with the F.A.A., Camp Grayling, and any other military bases in the Midwest to ask why these Air Force jets had flown over northern Michigan.

I know an Air Force military jet when I see one. To this day, the F.A.A. and the military claim there were absolutely no military aircraft in our area. That is a lie! I believe our government knows much more than they care to admit or explain to common folks.

I do not think this object was a military project either. People have suggested it was a military experimental aircraft, but I beg to disagree. We sent our video to NASA, whose engineers inspected it closely. Several of them actually called me and clearly stated the metal did not appear to be manmade.

The lady, Michael, and I remained close friends after this sighting. Despite the amazing incident and the positive changes we experienced in our own attitudes about life—we had some mixed feelings afterwards.

The experience changed each of us in different ways. We talked about it for many years. For instance, the lady, now my friend, chooses not to focus on the sky so much anymore. She is grateful to be living her life, here, now, day-to-day, and to be experiencing everything she has at the moment. She feels the incident and aftermath "grounded" her somehow.

Michael felt much as I do. We no longer look at ourselves the same way as we did before. I'm more tolerant, open, and appreciative of the world we live in. The Universe is so much bigger than I ever thought, and we are like little grains of sand. I now realize there is a higher purpose, a higher meaning in life that is difficult for man to comprehend. In fact, it's incomprehensible. The Universe goes beyond our minds, beyond our egos, and I am no longer as self-involved and self-absorbed as I once was. I watch and wonder more attentively now.

I still see those colors dancing in my head and I wish I could share them with people. Our universe has colors we've never seen before.

Trooper Glenn Guldner, Michigan State Police, Traverse City, Michigan
Note: Trooper Glenn Guldner is deceased.
The events he shared occurred several years ago.

The Encounter

I retired from the police force in 2002. The encounter occurred in the middle of the night in September 2008 at my home in a rural area near Holland, Michigan, which sits on the coast of Lake Michigan. It had been a warm, calm, uneventful evening; my family was in bed. The last thing I remember was watching TV on the couch.

The next thing I knew, I was standing in the yard outside my home. It was dark and absolutely quiet. I was not dreaming; I was completely conscious. The silence was eerie. Ahead in the near distance I saw a pin-size light, then all of a sudden a very bright wave-like flash that seemed to move through and pass me, almost knocking me back a step. I then felt a presence behind me. I turned around to see three small gray beings just standing there. Shoulder to shoulder.

They were the classic, gray, science-fiction-like aliens standing at a height of about four feet. They had large, black, almond-shaped eyes and long slender arms and legs. Oddly enough, I was not afraid. It was as if I recognized them or somehow knew them. I did not feel intimidated in the least.

The being in the middle said that they needed my help. His lips did not move; communication was telepathic. His request was the same as you'd hear from a friend or neighbor. I willingly agreed to help. Something happened, but I don't remember what it was. The next thing I remember is looking up and seeing a huge craft hovering. I see a second craft about four hundred feet away from the main one. I sense that time has passed since I first communicated with them but I can't tell how much.

I am now in a semi-paralyzed state; very, very tired, as though I had done a lot of work. I am breathing heavy and damp with perspiration. It takes all of my strength to just stand up. My arms hang down at my sides and as I am looking up at the craft I notice something out of the corner of my eye. Laboriously and with all the strength I can muster, I look to my left and realize there are two other men (humans) standing near me. We are about six feet apart from each other. They are also looking up. I do not know who they are. They look to be in their thirties. Neither of them seems able to talk or move either. They look as paralyzed and tired as me. They are breathing heavily as well and looking up. There isn't a sound to be heard or a breath of air moving.

A bright light at ground level is behind us and illuminates the area, including the craft hanging in the air; but I can not turn around to see the source. I then realized that the small gray beings are gone.

The next thing I remember is looking up at the craft in the night sky. There is a thunderous sound and an opening two- to three-hundred-feet wide appears in the sky. It is amazing! I can  see blue sky and clouds through the opening—but it is still night time where I stand. Clouds are "turning into themselves" around the opening. I can think of no other way to explain it; the clouds are "turning into" themselves around the opening which is round. Then, in the blink of an eye, the largest craft flies into the opening, followed instantly by the second ship. Then the sky closes up.

Again I hear a loud clap of thunder. With that, I awaken from this strange state and find myself inside the house. However, my eight-year-old daughter is now sleeping on the living room floor, which is weird. What the hell just happened to me? I wonder. I grab my kids' crayons and start drawing what I saw.

I notice it is about 5:30 A.M. At this point, I'm in a daze and a normal morning starts shortly thereafter. My wife goes to work, my daughter to school, and I don't share my experience with anyone yet. As usual, my wife calls me from work later that day. She tells me that our daughter woke up in the middle of the night, around three-thirty, and saw a lot of bright flashing lights outside our upper roof dormer window. My wife told her to go back to bed but instead our daughter went to sleep on the living room floor. My jaw dropped to the floor when my wife told me this because I had not said anything to her about what had happened to me. I had received confirmation that my encounter had really happened.

Later, I talked with my daughter about that night and she said she saw about eleven flashes of light. That's all she counted before she got scared and put her head underneath the covers. She waited a little while before looking again and, when she didn't see the lights anymore, she ran up to tell my wife.

If my daughter awoke between three and three-thirty and I found myself back inside the house at five-thirty, what happened to me during those two plus hours? Why did I feel so tired? And, most importantly, why couldn't I remember anything in between? I was sick with flu-like systems for a week after, which was odd because I seldom get the flu—especially at the end of summertime.

I filed a report with The Mutual UFO Network (MUFON) and they have been supportive and helpful. MUFON said that I'm one of only a few people who remember the hole in the sky. They also said it's not unusual to only remember the beginning and the ending of such an experience.

Two scientists came up from Detroit and Indianapolis to do

exhaustive testing and a complete search of my property. They inspected a small tree in the backyard that dropped dead only one week later. They also found some plants dying off and they took soil and leaf samples. I have not heard anything back as of this time. I believe the investigation is still ongoing.

There isn't a day or an hour that goes by when I don't think about this. The experience doesn't run my life but I am constantly playing the incident over in my mind. This was an extraordinary experience, one I never thought would happen to me; but it did and my life will never be the same.

Afterward I was driven to make a model of the UFO and I also designed a rudimentary picture of the hole in the sky (see image on page 184). The photo below is of the model I made to depict what I saw. The craft had vein-like lines going around the outside of the main sphere. These red veins had a glossy appearance. The two smaller white globes on the ends of the beams seemed to glow slightly.

Not Ready to Go

The police department I used to work for is located in a small historical town in southwestern Michigan. We would have occasional drug traffic on I-94 between Chicago and Detroit, but otherwise it was a quiet, uneventful retirement community.

One morning, my partner and I were called to a natural death at an elderly lady's home. The well-kept house was decorated with lavender Swiss-like shutters and surrounded by aromatic, colorful flowerbeds. I remember thinking what a pleasing place this would be to live.

When we entered the upstairs bedroom, we found several of the lady's relatives gathered sweetly around her bed, grieving and saying beautiful things about her and the life she had led.

My partner had investigated many natural death situations before, but this was my first. Although she looked peaceful, she was obviously deceased. I checked her pulse carefully, just as a matter of showing concern. She lay under the bed covers, wearing a soft paisley nightgown, with one hand on her heart— an unforeseen victim of a heart attack. We were told she was an active, spirited member of the community and highly vivacious. Although almost eighty, no one expected her to go this soon. I chuckled at the spicy romance novel sitting on the nightstand.

Her body was stiff to the touch and her face was an ash gray with deep lines indicating a joyful, happy life. I could tell she liked to smile. As usual, I lifted the bed covers to make sure nothing about the death appeared suspicious.

While my partner continued taking notes, I phoned the coroner. The lady's daughter went downstairs to get us some coffee and give us space. We didn't object. It was a kind, warm environment. We were in no hurry to leave.

My partner bent over the body, to check the carotid artery for a pulse once more—a standard operating procedure. I commented, "She's been dead over an hour. I don't know why we always overstress this crap."

At that moment, the dead lady's hand slipped off her chest and her chin and chest rose, as if to clear an airway from her throat to her heart. She took a deep, powerful breath, and then exhaled with seemingly deliberate intent! The breath was commanding, quick, and authoritative. We both jumped back in shock. My partner dropped his pen and let out a suppressed shriek and said, "Oh *shit!* She's still *alive!*" His expression was priceless. I'm sure mine was, too.

After a few seconds of stunned silence, reality set in, and I regained my composure. Defiantly I leaned over her and said, "Bullshit. You are dead. This *ain't funny!*" and inspected her face more closely. It is not unusual for a dead body to let out gases and carbon dioxide, though this incident seemed well after the fact. According to the family it had been at least an hour since she died. I started to think the time line that they gave us was wrong.

No sooner had I finished talking when the dead lady suddenly took another desperate gasp for more air—sending me springing backwards in alarm, like a scared kitten, nearly tripping on my shoes. I thought *this is far from normal!*

I exclaimed, "Holy shit! This is crazy. She is dead. This ain't right." And then she took another frantic distressed heave for air. I thought, *She's trying to resume her life again—or give me a heart attack!*

"It's-it's like she's trying to *jump start* herself back to life," my partner gasped. It was as if he had just read my mind.

She took a third breath, but discontinued in the middle of it. Then, as suddenly as she inhaled those two and a half breaths, she abruptly stopped. She exhaled and rested forever—as if realizing it was no use, too late, her death forlornly inevitable.

My partner felt the same way I did. There was no reasonable explanation for the occurrence. The account is what it is.

My partner and I left the room and indulged in a cup of decaffeinated coffee, wishing it were Jack Daniels, as we politely, but awkwardly, talked with the family members downstairs. We mentioned nothing about the incident, though I did kindheartedly affirm she must have been a determined old soul who loved life to its fullest. My partner added, "I don't know exactly why, but I feel that way, too."

The Amazing Shot

My most memorable spiritual experience as a police officer occurred in 1990, when I was a member of the state police Emergency Support Team (E.S. Team). We are the crisis managers of the agency and called upon whenever there are barricaded gunmen involved or very dangerous situations that require extra support or specially trained personnel.

My team was requested to assist on a domestic violence incident. The situation had already escalated to two deputies down (both shot and lying behind their patrol cars bleeding) and a woman whose right arm was nearly blown off and who was bleeding to death inside her house. Her seventy-five-year-old husband, Gordon, had Alzheimer's disease and had shot all of them. He would not allow police to take his wife, though he did let EMS inside. They applied a tourniquet to the woman's arm, but she was gradually fading away.

As a team we decided we would take a life in order to save a life. This was the first time the E.S. Team had ever made this decision. The team leader, therefore, was reluctant. Though the plan sounded callous, the man's wife was bleeding to death. Once the man was shot, the entry team could go into the house and extricate the woman to safety.

The lady was dying and our negotiation tactics were failing, so I volunteered to be the shooter. I was one of the best shots on the team. I could accurately shoot seven out of ten .12-gauge shotgun primers at fifty yards, with only a 4-power optical scope! I was good. (Primers are one-eighth of an inch in size.)

I grabbed my 30.06 rifle and got into position. The plan was to call out to Gordon over the P.A. system, wait for him to cup his hands around his eyes, and then shoot him between the eyes when he looked out. He had already looked out the window like this several times. The front door had two long, narrow windows, each about eight inches wide, which are common on trailer front doors.

We called to Gordon over the P.A. and, as anticipated, he cupped his hands and looked out the narrow window. I looked through my riflescope, had a perfect shot, but suddenly I couldn't do it. I saw his elderly innocent eyes, his face—it was like looking at my grandfather! I lowered my gun and my spotter said, "What's the matter?"

I was somewhat stunned. I lied and said, "My scope fogged up." I raised my rifle again. During this moment of compassion and indecisiveness, I prayed to God that I wouldn't have to kill this man.

However, a formal decision had been made for me to shoot him between the eyes. My prayer and my actions were contradictory. I reminded myself that our intent was to save the woman inside, so I aimed at the man's head and took the shot. The man fell back. He never jumped, flinched, or turned.

When the shot was fired, my scope and vision was dead-on Gordon's forehead above the bridge of his nose. I did not shake or shank the shot. The bullet hole in the window is proof. The hole shows where I aimed. If Gordon were standing upright again, the bullet hole was placed exactly between his eyes. And the shape of the hole shows the bullet went straight in.

However, the bullet actually hit his right shoulder, far away from his head. He lived! This is a bizarre and unexplained mystery. The crime lab went to the scene and measured. There is no explanation as to how the bullet hit Gordon's shoulder instead of killing him. The bullet experts could not explain how it happened, given the nature of the shot. The bullet hole in the window clearly went through the center of the window at eye level—and squarely! To hit his shoulder, the bullet hole would have had to have been lower and to the left.

Because police always want definitive explanations, several officers suggested that I just shanked the shot; but even they know that didn't make any sense. The bullet hole in the window clearly shows I didn't shank it. If I had shanked it, the hole would be in a different place.

God answered my prayer and moved the bullet. There is no other explanation. God, through the power of His own Law, can do anything. And this time he defied the law of physics. The bullet must have moved after it went through the window even though, physically, we think this is impossible. Witnesses know Gordon never jumped up or swung his shoulder into the bullet.

Interestingly, immediately after the shooting, I could only see black and white. My eyes could not distinguish colors. Dr. Kaufmann, our departmental psychologist, said that I was in psychological denial because I didn't want to hurt anybody.

I think my temporary color blindness was a symbolic message from God as well. After this incident, my vision about life changed from black and white to color, and so dramatically! This temporary visual impairment was indicative of the change in my spirit. I became more thankful, more grateful, and more spiritually courageous.

An Electrical Guest

I woke up in the middle of the night during a thunderstorm. I couldn't get back to sleep so I got up for a drink of water and then lay back down in bed, eyes wide open. A small night-light enabled me to see everything in the room, including a beloved photo of an old mystic hanging on the wall. My parents taught me to love thunderstorms; they usually relax me. I lay in bed and watched Mother Nature's electric show.

Suddenly a ball of dancing lights came through my open bedroom window and stopped about four feet in front of me. I was so shocked I couldn't move. It looked like Christmas tree tinsel chopped up in tiny, elongated pieces. It was about two feet high and two feet wide. As it flickered and crackled in front of me it emitted a sound like squealing rats. "E-e-e-e-e-e!" it screamed.

A wave of fear raced through me. Instinctively I thought, *This is electricity! I could get electrocuted! This is not a good situation!* I looked at the copper jewelry hanging on the wall next to me and wondered *Is copper a conductor of electricity?* Then I gripped the wooden sideboards on my bed and thought, *I sure hope this wood grounds me!*

The ball of light hovered in front of me for about seven seconds. It seemed to look right at me as I clung—*frozen*—to the wooden bed frame. An arm of it reached for the copper; then it appeared to change its mind before exiting out my bedroom door! It left as fast as it had come.

When my autonomic nervous system finally settled down and I could breathe again, I assured myself I was awake and that I was totally sober. I got up for another drink of water and, eventually, went back to sleep.

In the morning my boyfriend, Bill, came over. I hesitated to say anything to him about the ball of lights, wondering if he'd believe me. He tends to be conservative. As he was flipping through the Sunday paper, I said, "Honey, I saw something really weird last night."

Half-interested, he said, "Yes? What happened?" as he continued to scan the paper for an interesting article.

Instead of hem-hawing along, I blurted, "A ball of lights came through my bedroom window last night—when it was thundering and lightning outside. This ball was huge! It hovered and flickered right in front of me. It started to . . ."

Suddenly Bill let go of the paper, leaned forward, and said,

"Did it make a sound? Did it go 'E-e-e-e-e-e'?" He looked as white as a ghost!

I was stunned. He had made the *exact* sound of the phenomena, without my prompting him.

I exclaimed, "That's the sound it made! *How did you know?*"

He said, "I saw that same thing when I was little boy in Kentucky. I believe it's the aftereffects of lightning. Very few people ever see this, let alone see it *inside* the house. You've seen something that only one in a million people get to see!" His voice grew thoughtful. "Like when you throw a stone in the water and then the waves come out . . . that was a wave of electricity after lightning hit!"

I was surprised and excited Bill knew what I was talking about. I also shared with him that I thought it seemed to be some sort of intelligent being; I swore it looked at me.

I decided to phone the television station and speak with the meteorologist on staff. At first he did not take me seriously; but after I explained who I was, he listened more intently. Unfortunately he had no explanation for the phenomena. He thought it could have been static electricity. I said, "No way. It didn't look like static. It looked like needles lit up; like a gigantic cluster of cut-up Christmas tinsel. And it made a very obvious sound." He said he wished I had videotaped it.

I finally said thank you, hung up, and thought, The media is just like attorneys. They want proof, everything presented to them on a silver platter . . . oh, whatever! I know what I saw, and Bill knew too.

Burnt Offerings

I was only thirty yards away when the subject saw me. It was only by chance that he did. A porch light came on at a house on Junction Street in response to my partner's gunfire. When he turned momentarily in response, his eyes fell on me. I could see in the look that the shock nearly turned him to stone. His throat erupted in a primal scream of rage—or was it fear? I knew at that moment that never before in his life had he felt the humiliation of that emotion. He tossed away the rifle he held in his hands and bolted.

Even as he coursed along the fence row, his legs pumping furiously, I put myself in his mind and could almost hear his thoughts. *How had this happened?* He'd no doubt been chortling in self-satisfaction over being able to find my partner and me sitting unsuspecting in the unmarked scout car, and to sneak up—so he thought—behind us so easily. Then I came upon him from behind, found him in the dark. *Why, by the blood of Zarabanda, didn't I feel him approach?* I could almost hear him shout. But he must have forced the distracting thoughts aside, because he pelted furiously toward Junction, with me in close pursuit.

A fence enclosed the western end of the field he'd been hiding in, so I doubted he would head that way: a man might climb a fence when he came to it, but it would slow him down. I sensed that he would head toward Junction. I was right. As I lurched into stride and raced after him, I heard more shots reverberate from the direction of Merritt Street, where my partner apparently engaged an accomplice. No matter now. Nothing I could do. The chase was on.

The subject emerged from the field and ran onto Junction.

He crossed the street and continued eastward on Merritt, skirting another warehouse on that side of the street. I was only twenty paces behind. But I wasn't young anymore. At forty-three, my wind was no good. He began to pull ahead.

I was still only thirty paces behind when he reached the far corner of the warehouse and turned left. In the time it took to take two breaths, I reached the corner behind him. Despite my ragged breathing, I grinned with satisfaction. I knew this building, and I knew that the subject had fled into a blind alley—there was no outlet, the high walls of the storage buildings rose on all sides. The alley ended in an impenetrable wall of cement. He was trapped.

As I paused at the corner of the building for the barest fraction of a second, I eased my head past the brick façade just far enough to peer with one eye down the alley. I was stunned. The cul-de-sac was deserted. The subject was gone! I thought at first that my eyes were deceiving me. I looked again, my whole head emerging from behind the wall. Nothing. I stepped quickly out and walked warily down the alley, my .357 Magnum revolver at the ready. Had some workman left a door ajar, permitting the subject to escape into a building? What rotten luck! But no, as I remembered, there were no doors, just the walls of the buildings . . . and the roofs were twenty feet in the air.

I walked all the way to the end of the alley, my eyes searching every corner and crevice. There were no parked cars. There were no trash dumpsters. There were no stacks of crates. The alley stood as clean and empty as an airplane hangar. There could be no mistake: the subject had simply vanished.

I holstered my weapon and stood for a moment in the darkness of the alley, the silence filling me. The cold, the sense of malignancy, were gone. But a trace of something intangible lingered in the air; a faint smell, so ethereal that I wasn't sure it was really there. I sought it, tried to identify it, finally lost it. I let the quiet and the silence fill me completely. After a while, I smiled.

I finally walked away, returning to Merritt Street and my partner, who was thankfully alive and uninjured after a shoot-out with one of the subject's associates.

Only when a lieutenant and an inspector arrived, took charge of the homicide scene, made notifications, and started asking questions, did I break out of my reverie and start talking to Magaly, the New York City magazine reporter who had been riding along with my partner and me for over a week.

"Where have you been?" she asked, breathless, her hair disheveled. She was completely out of sorts over the shooting she'd witnessed only moments earlier.

"Chasing someone," I said. "Chasing our guy. It was *him*. I know it. But he's gone. He got away. Disappeared."

Looking into her eyes, I could tell it was impossible for her to gauge my mood. She finally said, "Well, it's dark. It'd be easy to lose someone . . . I guess it happens, huh?"

"No, I mean he *disappeared*," I insisted. "He just vanished, Maggie. He ran down a dead-end alley. I had him. I really had him. He was cornered. Then he was . . . *gone*."

"Well, he couldn't just—"

"He did." I turned again and looked into the night. "He did."

Maggie shivered. "It's him, then," she murmured. As you say, Bill. It's *him*."

I quietly nodded.

Before the arrival of the homicide team, the lieutenant, with the consent of the inspector, took initial steps to preserve evidence and organize the scene. First, I ordered a scout car crew to go back up to the vacant lot where I had discovered the subject hiding and secure the area. They quickly found the rifle the subject had thrown away, nestled among some weeds. They let the weapon lay where they found it, and waited impatiently for it to be photographed, measured, and ultimately retrieved and tagged by responding evidence technicians.

Next, the lieutenant requested a K-9 unit to come out to the scene to attempt a track of the subject. The dog handlers arrived within a few minutes and were directed to the waiting officers along the fence line in the vacant lot. The dog, a big German shepherd, immediately picked up a scent from the ground, as well as from the rifle. He pulled eagerly at his leader and struggled against the leash, pulling his handler along at a trot. "Find him, Rocky," urged the handler, a young cop whom, Magaly said, looked like Andy Garcia. "Find him, boy!"

The dog followed a strong scent all along the route I'd taken in pursuit of the subject, all the way into the dead-end alley, and down to its end. The dog sniffed nervously along the blank wall for a moment and then sat on its haunches, staring straight ahead—it was trained to do that after locating the person it was looking for. Rocky was doing his job. "There," he was saying. "There he is—in the wall."

I never saw the subject again, and no arrests were ever made.

Excerpt from *Burnt Offerings* by Charles W. Newsome, Detroit Police Department, Retired.

The Lost Badge

A young Canadian conservation officer in Sault Ste. Marie, Canada, shared the following experience with me as I was crossing the border into Michigan. I noticed he wasn't wearing a badge on his jacket and curiously inquired about it. He pulled his badge from his pocket and stated, "See, I do have a badge, but let me tell you what happened." He then relayed this extraordinary story . . .

I wanted to kick myself. What kind of a police officer loses his badge? But that is what I'd done. And, in the middle of the woods, of all places! I searched and searched, but it was a losing battle. The thick layer of fallen bark and leaves was an ideal place for a badge to remain hidden. Every time I thought I saw something, shadows would move across the ground, revealing that what I had seen was only a glint of light filtering down through the leaves. Nevertheless, I returned to the woods the next day and the next, each time retracing my steps, even getting down on my hands and knees . . . but to no avail. It looked like I would have to break down and report the loss of my most treasured possession.

Reluctantly, I decided I would make a report today; after all, somebody else might find it and use it illegally to impersonate a police officer. My cheeks burned as I thought about the ribbing I would get from everybody in the Ontario Provincial Police Department when they learned that I had lost my badge.

But an unexpected assignment prevented me from sitting at my desk and writing up my report. A severe storm had ripped through the northernmost section of Ontario, more than one hundred miles away, and I was asked to travel there to report on the extent of the damage. I still hadn't given up on my badge, and as I drove north I said a prayer that I would find it.

When I arrived at the designated area, I found the forest was terribly distressed after the storm. Old mossy trees, pines, limbs, and brush had fallen everywhere chaotically. It looked as though the wind had lifted most of the trees up and thrown them down into a pile of debris. I noticed an eagle's nest had toppled, and the tree in which it had been built was nearly upended. What if there were baby eagles in the nest? I felt a strong urge to investigate. If there were birds in it, I could transfer them to a wildlife refuge.

Carefully I picked my way through black timber, rocks, fallen trees, and brush, climbing and tripping as I made my way awkwardly through the devastated landscape. I expected the worst—the mother dead and her eaglets injured, starved, thirsty, perhaps the whole family *dead*.

To my surprise, the nest was empty! I sifted through the leaves and bark—mother and babies had vacated the nest, and there was not a sign of disaster to the family. Relieved, I stepped back to admire how well the nest was put together and how cleverly constructed. This was the first time I had seen an eagle's nest close up. Just the fact it had come down *intact* seemed a miracle. And that's when I glimpsed something *shiny* sparkling through the leaves and sticks. I picked into the lining of the nest, and there, nestled safely inside, was my *badge!*

For a moment, I couldn't believe it. To say that I was astounded would be an understatement. I thought I was dreaming. The eagle had recognized a treasure and carried it to the safest place she knew, her home. And I, concerned about the safety of her children, had found it. What was the likelihood of such a sequence of events being just coincidence? How was it that I was the person chosen to drive one hundred miles to a forest previously unknown to me? If the eagle had not found my badge and carried it off for safe-keeping, perhaps I might never have seen it again. And why did I feel such an *urge* to look inside the nest? What humbled me the most was the complex series of steps I was led to take. And I didn't even know it when I took them!

The Kid

Abandoned mines are extremely dangerous to explore and even to go near. In Utah, many are undocumented, especially on private property. Mine shafts are particularly hazardous because they are nothing but vertical openings that go very deep, some more than one thousand feet into the earth. People can fall into the shafts never to be found again, which makes abandoned mines and mine shafts ideal places to dump dead bodies.

I am an undercover narcotics officer. A confidential informant told me that a body had been dumped down a winze of an abandoned mine shaft. Winzes are vertical drops; but within the mines themselves they are shafts that connect one level to another lower level, like an elevator shaft without the elevator. Winzes can descend to depths that are water-filled, toxic, and radioactive. I'm sure bodies can decompose quickly if culprits know what they are doing. (I do not recommend anyone ever explore such places. The shaft collars of these dormant mines are often loose and unconsolidated and the sides of the walls break away easily from intrusion.)

I drive into the quiet countryside and get permission from the owner to investigate the abandoned mine on his property. I first search for any disturbances in the area—such as loose gravel, footwear impressions, and blood—anything to indicate that a body was dumped. I don't see anything unusual. What I do find are old equipment, piles of waste rock all around, and a couple of old buildings left standing. I spot what I believe to be a mine tunnel, wide open. At least this is consistent with what the informant told me. You can't always trust an informant's information.

I shine my light through the mine opening and see movement in a dark corner. It appears to be a child, about four feet tall. I immediately yell to him, "Police, come out! You are not in any trouble! It is too dangerous for you to go any farther! Hello?" There is no answer.

I think it might be the rancher's kid, but learn later he didn't have any children. This is a desolate area and it doesn't appear like anyone has been here in a long time—not even vehicles.

Reluctantly, I step into the opening of the mine. I do not intend to proceed much farther. It is too dangerous. The opening is held up by old support timbers that seem safe enough and stable but could easily be rotted wood. I try not to be fooled by appearances. Such old structures can easily disintegrate from the weight of just one person

"Young man," I said, "this is NOT a cave! It is unstable and can cave-in! Come out!" I am anxious for the boy to walk out as I know the dangers of these places. Still, no answer. I walk into the mine a little farther, and I see movement again. "I see you! Come out! I just want to talk to you. You can DIE if you fall down a hidden shaft!"

There is no answer—yet I know I am not seeing things. It has to be a kid. It moved on two legs and appeared agile. He moved quickly. I was certain the kid was playing games with me. Then I thought to myself, Okay, I'll just be totally still and catch you on your way out. Then I'll give you a good scolding and send you home.

I stand behind a support beam for what felt like an hour; in reality, it was probably only twenty minutes. It was a hot day and time felt like it was standing still. A flicker of movement: I see the shadow again.

But as soon as I see it, it disappears. And I swear I didn't move a muscle. I start to second-guess myself and think, Well, it could be an animal. Maybe it is a bear or a mountain lion and is merely escaping the noon heat. After all, animals are known to den in these mines. I keep one hand near my pistol at all times.

It must have been 100 degrees, even in the cooler recesses of the mine. I take a drink of water and it moves again. The shadow is definitely two-legged and there are two obvious long, slender arms. It is human alright, I think. I no longer doubt myself.

"Come on!" I shout. "I could use your help right now! Talk to me!" It moves swiftly again from one support structure to another. I can't see it clearly in the dark. I stand still for another twenty minutes. I decide to wait until it is close enough and then I'll shine my flashlight on him. Admittedly, I am hot, getting frustrated, irritated, and tired of waiting. Nevertheless, I remain motionless and unwavering. When I'm truly beginning to doubt myself, I finally see movement again, coming closer and closer. He was almost within arm's reach; I had him now! I surprised him. I shined my light on him in one swift click of the button. When he turned toward me, I saw a reptilian-faced creature that scared the shit out of me—and I ran!

The instant the light shone on its face, it dove into the earth like it was water. Initially I thought he went into a winze, but there was not an opening. It was solid ground.

I wasn't seeing things. Its face was greenish-gray and reptilian. Maybe it was an animal; but no one has been able to convince me of that yet. It was too weird!

Turn the page. On a scale of one to ten—with ten being perfect—I rate the accuracy of my memory at 8.5. I suppose it could have been a person in a mask, but in a dark mine? With no one else around?

Flying Free

I was dispatched to an accident on a country road about five miles out of town. A sixth-grade teacher on her way home from school ran over an eleven-year-old boy on a go-cart. She was driving fifty-five miles an hour.

The child's family lived on a hundred acres that were intersected by the highway. His parents bought him a go-cart and built him a track. Half of the track was on one side of the road, while the other half was on the other side. They instructed their son to always stop before crossing the road. He promised to observe this rule.

Unfortunately, this fatal evening, the boy forgot to stop and look before crossing. He was hit by an innocent motorist and apparently was thrown from the go-cart.

When I arrived at the scene, the driver of the vehicle, a middle-aged woman, was frantic and hysterical. She started running to a nearby field. "He's over there! He's over there! I saw him go over there! I saw him fly from his go-kart into the field! Oh, God. He must be okay. He must be," she sobbed.

The teacher darted into the field, just off the roadway, and I obediently followed close behind her.

"He's over here!" she called. "I know he is! He's somewhere in these bushes." We began running in circles . . . round and round . . . nonstop. We could barely keep our breath. The lady, now delirious, kept saying over and over again, "He's got to be here . . . he's got to be. I *saw* him fly over my windshield. He's here . . . I know he is."

Suddenly I had a horrific thought. It somehow wound its way through my own confused and anguished mental state. I said,

"Stop!" At first she didn't seem to hear me. I ordered her again, "STOP! This is insane! Stop running!"

She was panting. I was panting. I listened to my inner thought, now coming through as clear as day. *The boy is under the car.* I looked to the roadway and at the teacher's car and said, "He is not here. He is under the car." We proceeded to walk back toward the road.

She protested, "But, but . . . but . . . I saw him *fly* into the field! He can't be under the car. He was here . . . he flew over there!" And she pointed behind us.

As I already intuitively knew, the boy *was* under the car. He was dead, probably killed instantly. I do not, however, believe the lady *imagined* seeing the boy fly into the field. I think what she saw was the boy's soul departing his body. He was struck so fast and with such force that he flew out of his body instantly.

Looking back, I realize we always have a choice to buy into another person's energy. We were running around in circles like maniacs—until I took control and said, "No. This doesn't feel right." When I quieted myself, then a clear message was able to come through.

Sometimes police troopers buy into energy, just like other people, but we have to learn to listen for spiritual guidance even more closely during emergencies and tragedies. Angels can't help us if we don't listen.

Swimming Out-of-Body

One early morning in late October, Central Dispatch received several 911 calls from various Lake Leelanau residents. People could hear a man screaming for help across the lake. I stopped at one of the residences to look, listen, and better pinpoint the man's position. Although I could hear him, it was still dark, so I used my flashlight to scan the water.

I finally located the distressed man in the water about one hundred yards from shore. He was barely clinging to his capsized fishing canoe and still screaming. He had been doing so for at least forty-five minutes. Without any further delay, I dropped my gun belt and stepped into the frigid water. I was an excellent swimmer, having grown up in South Florida, but this was different. Not only was the water freezing, I was also wearing a polyester uniform, a bulletproof vest, and black boots that added weight and discomfort to my rescue efforts.

The man kept yelling, "Help me! Hurry up! I can't last much longer! H-E-E-L-L-P M-E-E-E-E!"

Because my adrenaline had kicked in, I finally shouted back crossly, "Shut the hell up! I'll be there in a minute!" I ripped off as many unneeded items as possible and started to walk toward the man. I thought to myself, *Piece of cake. I won't have to swim too far, this is shallow water* . . . Then, without warning, I went from chest deep to sinking to above my chin before catching myself and treading water. The drop-off was so unexpected I accidentally inhaled freezing water.

My body went into shock. It felt like someone had squeezed my chest until it was the size of a ping-pong ball. I had never had an out-of-body experience until now! My whole respiratory system stopped, just like that, and I could see myself treading water. For a few seconds I became the panic itself.

I can hardly describe what it felt like when gallons of ice-cold water started to fill up my uniform. I was shocked that my boots floated, while my vest weighted down my chest. My arms were already going numb, but I started dog paddling. I splashed and kicked backwards until I reached shallow water again. (God sure gives us some excellent survival instincts.) Then, I stood up. I still felt separate from my body and was trying to recompose my bearings and thoughts. I said to myself, *"Now get it together. You threw your own wrench in the situation by not being careful. Regain your faculties and swim out there again! It's okay. Just slow down.*

Sometimes I don't know if these are actually my own thoughts or if God is talking to me. I finally thought, *Okay* and then started swimming towards the man.

I noticed the yelling had been reduced to small, intermittent, helpless yelps with long intervals in between. I was concerned he was going to go under. No sooner had I reached him when he passed out. This was a good thing, actually! I knew I wouldn't have to combat any resistance as I towed the man back to shore.

It was exhausting! Visually, the distance seemed far, but water is illusive. Somehow, recruit school training cannot match what you actually feel in a survival situation. For a big guy who works out, this was one of the most physically challenging feats I'd attempted. When we got to shore, I was so tired and cold that everything seemed dream-like and seemed to be moving in slow motion. It was weird seeing life like a dream!

At first I was so relieved to be on shore. *Thank God! I made it to shore and I see people! Someone will help me now!* I could see fire trucks and EMS personnel scurrying about, but then realized nobody was coming to assist me. I could hardly stand up, let alone drag the man any further!

Suddenly I see a huge piercing light and am blinded! It was

still dark out and the bright light stunned me. I carefully dropped the fisherman to the ground and stared blankly into the light.

No, it was not an I-see-the-light-I-must-be-going-to-heaven situation, I was just confused. It took me a few seconds to see clearly. I was in shock. As I adjusted my eyes, I saw a volunteer rescue worker just standing there, shining his blazing flashlight at me, only inches from my face.

I yelled at him, "Damn it! I've already *seen the light once*, go grab us some blankets!" I probably shouldn't have been so hard on the young fellow. He was apparently very new to his job.

When I got home, I peeled off my uniform and I learned that polyester is the worst material to swim in because it retains every molecule of water possible and no heat whatsoever. It took me three days to feel warm again.

The man did survive and fully recovered from the incident. I was awarded a Medal of Honor by the Michigan Sheriff's Association.

UFO Sighting

On January 8, 1956, I was stationed at Wurtsmith Air Force Base, in East Tawas, Michigan, working as a road trooper on night patrol. My partner, Max Waterbury, had talked to me about UFOs just days before this incident, which I thought was eerily ironic. He said anyone who believed in UFOs was crazy and should be put in a mental ward.

At the beginning of our shift, we stopped for coffee at the local restaurant near the state dock. East Tawas is located on Lake Huron, one of the five Great Lakes.

Our lunch was interrupted with a telephone call from the desk sergeant at our post. Wurtsmith Air Force Base had called the state police post to request that troopers check on a large object that had been hovering about 2,000 feet above Strawberry Marsh. The air base had it on its radar and had been watching the object for the past half hour. The military officer was excited but concerned and asked us to take a look.

Max and I hurried back to the post to pick up a few things, including a rifle that Max grabbed out of the closet. I looked at Max and said, "I thought you didn't believe in unusual objects or little green men. What if they're friendly?"

He just rolled his eyes and we left.

Strawberry Marsh, a rural deserted area with two-tracks and unoccupied hunting camps this time of year, is halfway between East Tawas and Oscoda. The snow was at least two feet deep. I plowed and barreled our patrol car through drifts and undulating terrain, until we finally rested in a three-foot snow bank.

In my trooping era, whoever got the car stuck had to shovel it out. The right front wheel seemed to be the side that was hung up. I was bent down and shoveling a combination of snow and wet gravel, when Max, who was standing in back of me, excitedly exclaimed, "LOOK AT THAT!"

I turned around, looked up, and then dropped the shovel in surprise. My eyes were nearly blinded. In the clear night sky, I observed a huge oval-shaped light fringed in red and green floating above the snow-capped tree lines. It appeared to be hollow, but wasn't. We were shocked.

We knew that if this object was hovering at 2,000 feet, as the military radar operator explained, then it had to be *massive*. It looked to be fifty feet wide from the 45° angle we observed it from. We couldn't believe our eyes. It wasn't a beam of light, rather a brilliant, extremely bright light that illuminated everything below it. The stars were out, but no moon, which lent well to its brilliance and clarity.

I am a private pilot and have owned six different aircraft. This was no airplane of any kind. What we thought was so weird was the *silence*. It didn't make a sound. As we watched, it would move back into the tree line where we could barely see it, but then move forward again into our view. It was *huge*.

I grabbed the radio and talked to Trooper Warner Palmer, who was working the desk that night. Still shocked, I reported our encounter. I told him, "This thing is huge!"

Trooper Palmer sounded just as excited as I did, answering, "Right! I got the Wurtsmith Air Force Base holding on both lines. Your description is consistent with theirs!"

As the object disappeared behind the treetops—this time for good—I was able to successfully free our patrol car from the snow bank. The Base advised that they'd vectored a T-33 to investigate, so we headed straight back to the post. I typed up our report and left it on the front desk counter for the media to pick up in the morning.

We were not the only officers who saw it. Deputy Leon

Putnam from the Iosco County Sheriff Department had also seen an object from his patrol car that night. He had made a traffic stop and was writing notes inside his vehicle when the object illuminated the interior of his patrol car. He described it as a flaming basketball, however, hovering over the treetops. His description was not the same as ours.

My partner and I were told that the Air Force would never call troopers at the post again. Apparently, the traffic controllers who dispatched us were "pulled on the carpet" and got in serious trouble for having contacted us. When reporters from the local newspaper tried to interview the Commanding Officer, Colonel Taylor, he told them, "No comment." The military denies to this day that anything unusual happened. They denied ever sending a T-33 to investigate.

This incident occurred when all three major newspapers in Michigan—the *Free Press*, *The Detroit News*, and the *Times*—were on strike. I had hoped the sighting would reach the wire services, but it never did.

Later, Max humbly asked me, "So, what do you think that thing was?"

He never ridiculed UFOs again.

Recovery Under the Mackinac Bridge

In September 1989, a young woman was driving northbound on I-75, crossing the Mackinac Bridge from the Lower Peninsula to the Upper Peninsula of Michigan, in a late-model subcompact car. It was late at night, raining, and very windy. She lost control of the vehicle and veered from the inside lane of the divided roadway to the outside lane. Somehow the car jumped the guardrail and traveled over the side of the bridge structure. The car and driver fell 180 feet to the water below, where they quickly submerged and sank to the bottom of the Straits of Mackinac. Rescue boats searched the waters, but found no trace of the vehicle or driver.

At the time, I was assigned to the Michigan State Police Underwater Recovery Unit, and sent to meet with several other Unit members in Mackinaw City on the south end of the bridge.

The team arrived at Mackinaw City three days prior to the day of the recovery dive. We met with the State Police from the Cheboygan Post, DNR Marine Officers, U.S. Coast Guard, Bridge Authorities, and local law enforcement. The first objective was to brief everyone about the accident.

A strong wind continued to blow for the next two days, so we had time to recreate the accident scene and plan for the recovery attempt. On the third day the wind and waves had settled enough to start the recovery dive.

My assigned partner and I were the first two divers to make the descent to the bottom, 156 feet below. We had an approximate location from U.S. Coast Guard sonar, where they had placed a 500-pound concrete block on the bottom as near to the vehicle as possible. Divers used a line attached from the bridge railing where the car went over, to the concrete block on the bottom.

My dive partner and I started down the ascent/descent line towards the bottom. The current was flowing from east to west through the Straits at about four knots that morning. We turned on our dive lights at about sixty feet and continued our descent.

The bottom came into view from about ten feet above, and we started our search for the vehicle, with me making a 360° sweep at the end of a twenty-five foot length of line. I found some debris from the inside of the car lying on the bottom, but not the car. Our plan was to make the sweep and return to the dive boat even if the car was not located. Our time on the bottom was limited at that depth, and we would soon have to start our slow return to the surface.

However, my dive partner tied another length of line that he had to the first and set off on his own. I stayed at the concrete block and started checking my dive computer. Much to my surprise, I was running low on air and my tissue gases were nearing maximum levels. I gave the emergency signal by jerking the search line three times to recall my dive partner. But, the line was slack. I decided that I couldn't leave my partner because he might not be able to locate the line he left on the bottom and would likely have to make an emergency ascent to the surface. Due to the current, he would have been carried far from the dive boat and into the area where many civilian observer boats were riding around to watch the show.

I decided to swim to the end of the search lines to see if I could find him. Once there, I could see a dive light about thirty feet away. He had located the car, and had detached himself from the search line so he could reach it. I kept signaling him with my light, but it seemed like forever before he noticed and swam to me. I immediately started swimming back to the ascent line with my dive partner behind me. As I made the turn upwards at the concrete block I drew my last breath from my tank.

It was 115 feet to the first decompression station, where another diver was waiting with spare scuba tanks. I knew I couldn't make it that far and turned to my partner for his octopus regulator so we could buddy-breathe and make a safe ascent. I didn't know he had sacrificed his octopus regulator for an air hose to feed his dry suit (I was diving in a wet suit). The only option was to buddy-breathe using his one regulator. He took a breath and gave me the regulator. I was to take three breaths and give it back so he could take three breaths. The problem was that when I took three breaths I needed 300 to catch up. We buddy-breathed twice when I decided to take my chances and head to the surface as fast as I could. My dive partner tried to hold me back because of the danger making a "blow and go" emergency ascent.

Even before I left my dive partner, my lungs were burning and in pain. I knew I was in trouble. But, in a moment, the pain went away. I was beginning to lose consciousness. I felt quite peaceful. I was still headed for the surface and exhaling the expanding air in my lungs. I was thinking that I had finally "bought the farm"— my expression for dying. I was sure I was going to die—and I accepted this fate.

I kept my hand on the line as I continued my nearly unconscious ascent. I don't know how deep I was when I noticed the safety diver above me. I stopped when I reached him, but didn't have the ability to put the regulator he was holding in my mouth. So, he put it in my mouth and purged the water out so I could breathe. Fortunately, I had enough consciousness left to do that part.

Just as suddenly, I realized I wasn't going to die after all. The safety diver was on wire communications with the dive boat.

They had been worried about my partner and me because we were way beyond our time limit for the depth we were working in. I had to stay at the forty-foot level for what seemed to be a very long time to decompress. Finally, I was able to ascend to the thirty-foot stop, then twenty feet, ten feet and, at last, the surface.

I was extremely cold by that time and shivering uncontrollably. I was helped onto the dive boat and transferred to the Coast Guard Buoy Tender where I was put on oxygen. I was debriefed and taken below deck where I lay on a bed for a long time.

As I began to relive the incident, anger at my dive partner emerged. I wondered if I should have left him and tended to my own safety. But, Michigan State Police Officers are not trained that way, and the highly specialized underwater recovery team members are even more dedicated to each other. In defense of my dive partner, the water depth surely affected our judgment— and he did find the car. However, I believed he needlessly almost cost me my life.

The vehicle and driver were brought to the surface and transported back to Mackinaw City.

The question is: What did I take away from this experience? I didn't see any bright lights or a glimpse of life beyond death—no angels or spiritual beings met with me. I was just lost in thoughts of my past and convinced I had bought the farm. I thought about my family, but not in a how-are-they-going-to-get-along-with-me-gone way. They were part of my many thoughts. Maybe I wasn't far enough away from life at that point to see in that perspective.

I wasn't panicked either, just peaceful. I'm not sure where I was, but I can say that I'm not ready to experience near-death again. What I took with me was a new appreciation for the transient nature of our life on Earth. And the experience changed my priorities in life. We are too often overwhelmed by the "white noise" in everyday existence, and would do well to eliminate as much of it as possible. Life is not a condition to take for granted.

Over-all, I look back at the recovery dive under the Mackinac Bridge as a useful learning experience. It certainly changed my diving methodology. About three years later I retired from the State Police and became a Scuba Instructor. I'm quite sure that my eighteen years experience on the Michigan State Police Underwater Recovery Team, and especially that day in late September 1989, made me a better instructor. In my opinion that's a pretty good deal in life.

About the Author

INGRID P. DEAN has worked with the Michigan State Police for almost twenty years in a variety of capacities, including road patrol, polygraph, forensic art, major crime investigation, and teaching police officers. Presently, Ingrid is a detective sergeant for the Michigan State Police in Traverse City, Michigan.

She attended Northwestern Military Preparatory School in Mound, Minnesota, and graduated with honors and qualified to attend the Air Force Academy in Colorado Springs. As life would dictate, Ingrid elected to attend Wayne State University in Detroit instead, obtaining a Bachelor of Arts degree in Art. She lived and studied various aspects of the spiritual dimension at Sanatano Ashram, Pontiac, Michigan, for eight years, followed by time served in the military. Ingrid joined the Michigan State Police in 1989.

In 2008, she obtained a Master's Degree in Transpersonal Studies from Atlantic University in Virginia Beach, Virginia. Her research entailed the collection of true police experiences in the field of transpersonal studies, a school of psychology that encompasses the transcendent and spiritual dimensions of humanity. It is an academic discipline rather than a religious or spiritual movement.

About the Author

Detective Sgt. Dean is an artist, musician, and a teacher of meditation. She is a licensed polygraph examiner for the State of Michigan. A private pilot and certified Basic Scuba Diver (PADI), she resides in Traverse City, Michigan, with her dog, Agate.